Dear Marion,

This is signed with joy to a fellow pilgrim and sister in Christ and is sent to you through the kindness of our mutual friend, Helga Shaw.

May the Lord bless and encourage us as together we take this vicarious journey to the land He knew so well. Let's pause often to reaffirm the glorious truth — Jesus is Lord!

God bless you, Marion —

Shalom,
Bill Francis
10/20/97

PS — Have you ever been in a jeep??

"Pray for the peace of Jerusalem...."
Psalm 122:6

THE STONES CRY OUT

The Stones Cry Out

Text and Photographs by

William W. Francis

Published by
The Salvation Army
Literary Department
USA EASTERN TERRITORY

Library of Congress Catalog-in-Publication Data

Francis, William W.
The Stones Cry Out.

ISBN: 0-89216-097-7

Published by The Salvation Army, Literary Department (USA Eastern Territory).

Chapters 1,4,5,6,9,10,11,13,15,16,17,18 originally were published in a twelve-part series in the U.S.A. *The War Cry* (ISSN 0043-0234).
The first article appeared in the May 26, 1990 issue, and the last in the December 8, 1990 issue.

All photographs taken by the author using Canon AE-1 equipment.

Unless otherwise indicated, scripture quotations used in this book are from the New International Version (NIV) of the Bible. Copyright © 1973, 1978, 1984 by the International Bible Society. Published by Zondervan Bible Publishers.

Other scripture quotations are identified as KJV (King James Version) or RSV (Revised Standard Version) of the Bible.

Color maps by arrangement with World Bible Publishers, Inc. (pages iv, 114, 115, 116) and Hammond Incorporated (page 121).

Drawings of *Herod the Great's Temple Mount* (pages 118-119) and *Jerusalem in 30 A.D.* (page 120) by Leen Ritmeyer.

Time Chart of Bible History (pages 127-129) by arrangement with Hammond Incorporated.

Layout and design by Timothy Clark and William MacLean.

Printed in the United States of America by Dickinson Press Inc.

Dedication

THIS BOOK is dedicated, with love, to my wife, Marilyn. She is my companion and colleague in ministry and shares a love, respect and passion for the land of our Lord - *Eretz Israel*.

Palestine in New Testament Times

This map is printed with the permission of World Bible Publishers, Inc.

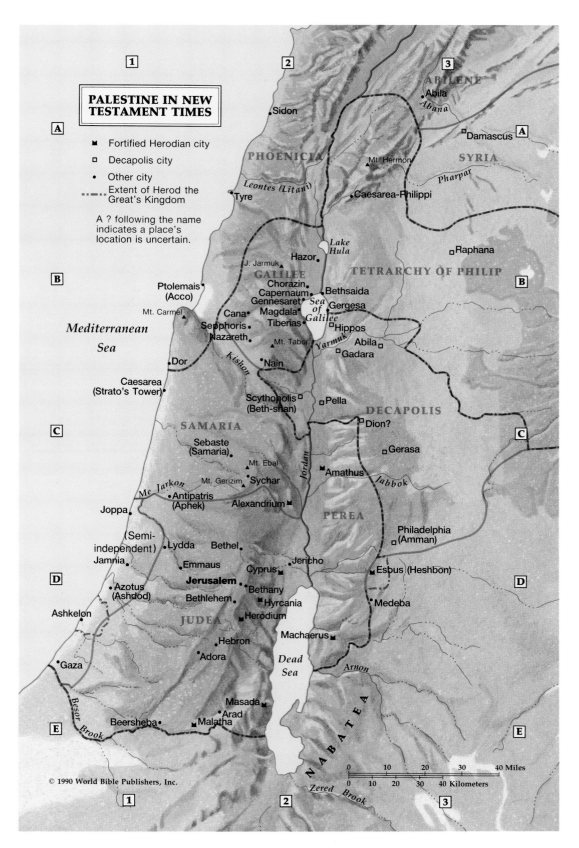

PALESTINE IN NEW TESTAMENT TIMES

- ◤ Fortified Herodian city
- ▫ Decapolis city
- • Other city
- ‑‑‑ Extent of Herod the Great's Kingdom

A ? following the name indicates a place's location is uncertain.

© 1990 World Bible Publishers, Inc.

When he came near the place where the road goes down the Mount of Olives, the whole crowd of disciples began joyfully to praise God in loud voices for all the miracles they had seen:

"Blessed is the king who comes in the name of the Lord!"

"Peace in heaven and glory in the highest!"

Some of the Pharisees in the crowd said to Jesus, "Teacher, rebuke your disciples!"

*"I tell you," he replied, "if they keep quiet, **the stones will cry out**."*

- Luke 19:37-40

Table of Contents

Acknowledgments

Reflecting on family and friends who influenced the writing of this book, I quickly realized that it would be impossible to thank all those who generously extended their encouragement, assistance and, most importantly, their prayers. To all those who said, "You should write a book" (or comparable counsel), I express my sincere gratitude.

I am particularly indebted to the following individuals, without whom the book would have remained an unfulfilled aspiration:

My wife, Marilyn, and children, Billy and Susan, for their inspiration, understanding and steady encouragement. They have been an endless source of strength and frequent antidote for discouragement. Their corporate resolve that I finish the book insured its completion.

Our esteemed international leader, General Eva Burrows, and my longtime friend and colleague, Dr. Roger J. Green, for their generous endorsements.

Salvation Army leaders who gave us the opportunity to host numerous tours to the Holy Land. A special word of appreciation goes to Commissioner Orval Taylor (R), whose vision afforded Salvationists and friends in the Eastern Territory (U.S.A.) the opportunity to travel to Israel, and to Commissioner Robert E. Thomson for giving his imprimatur to this book.

Our devoted Israeli guide and friend, Shabtai Levanon, for his enthusiastic support and invaluable advice. "Shep" is a true "Rabbi" to his many Gentile friends.

The Editor-in-Chief of the *The War Cry* (U.S.A.), Colonel Henry Gariepy, for first suggesting the twelve-part series carried in the *The War Cry*, and for his unique ability to spur on apprehensive writers.

Lt. Colonel William D. MacLean, Literary Secretary, who first suggested that *The War Cry* series be expanded into a book, and the members of the Eastern Territory's Literary Council for their patience, helpful suggestions and unending support.

My good friend and twice fellow pilgrim to the Holy Land, Captain Richard J. Munn, for his meticulous, candid and insightful scrutiny of the manuscript.

Winnie and Mervin Sedlar, for their careful proofreading of each chapter and the Miracles and Parables charts in the appendix.

Above all, I want to acknowledge the continuing grace and inspiration of our heavenly Father, without which this book never would have been written.

Foreword

A great preacher of yesteryear, the late Robert G. Lee, liked to tell of his first visit to the Holy Land. When he saw the Mount of Calvary, so great was his excitement that he started to run and soon outdistanced his party in climbing the hill. When at last the guide caught up with him, he asked, "Sir, have you been here before?" For a moment there was a throbbing silence. Then, in a whispered awe, Dr. Lee replied, "Yes, I was here, nearly two thousand years ago."

Indeed, the Holy Land casts that kind of a spell over every Christian. This land of destiny is unlike any other place in the world. We cannot but feel that we were a part of what happened in that ancient land. The Lord's Advent and mighty life became the hinge of history on which the whole world, our very loves and eternal destiny turn.

Thus a journey to the Holy Land is always far more than a tour or a visit. It is a pilgrimage of the soul. Its towns and country roads pulsate with the remembered presence of the Lord. Its sites and shrines evoke scenes where God walked the earth in sandals, healed the sick, performed His mighty miracles and shared His incomparable teachings.

On one of Jerusalem's hills the Son of God poured out His life in infinite love for all the world. And from one of its tombs He rose triumphantly from the dead. The land of the Lord resonates with the Lord of the land. Indeed *its stones cry out,* and their message is eloquent and powerful.

William Francis brings us a compelling work that serves as a vicarious pilgrimage to the Holy Land. He has given us something far more than a mere geographical or descriptive text, although it is an insightful work. He has captured the spirit of the Holy Land and what it means to us.

William Francis has blended three great loves of his life to bring a work that is devotional as well as definitive.

First, William Francis loves the land of Israel. He has conducted tours there numerous times, has taught on the subject and has a rare and intimate knowledge of its spiritual history.

Second, William Francis loves the Lord. He, with his wife Marilyn, has dedicated his whole life in service to Jesus Christ.

Third, William Francis loves the Bible. He is an astute student, teacher and preacher of the Word.

The author, with literary skill and craftsmanship, has blended these three great loves into a presentation that will enlighten, enrich and inspire the reader.

The careful reader will also note on the dedication page a fourth great love of his life, one who has beautifully shared with him in the experience that has given birth to this book.

As Editor-in-Chief, I was grateful for the privilege to have introduced a portion of this series to the readers of The Salvation Army's national publication, *The War Cry*. The informative texts were enhanced with the beautiful color photos taken by the author, and we are pleased that this volume will be complemented with many of these same striking photos.

Reader, fasten your spiritual seat belt for this guided tour through the Holy Land. You will journey to the historical sites, holy shrines, archaeological digs and places associated with the life and ministry of our Lord. You will amble through the pastoral setting of Bethlehem and see the very spot believed to be where time was split in two. You will walk along the pebbled shore and by the azure blue waters of the Galilean Sea, nestled in the hills of Israel.

From the briny waters of the Dead Sea and the wilderness of Judea, you will climb up to Jerusalem, where history will come alive. On your pilgrimage Bethlehem, Nazareth, Tiberius, Capernaum, the Mount of Olives, Bethany, the Jordan River and other Bible settings will vibrate with new meaning.

You will stand in the room believed to have been where Jesus observed the Last Supper and where the Holy Spirit came at Pentecost. You will walk amid the ancient olive trees in Gethsemane, trudge up the narrow cobblestone road of the Via Dolorosa where Christ carried His cross to Calvary. You will stand in reverence before the site of Calvary and enter in awe the tomb where Christ was buried. When you finish this fascinating and inspiring tour with William Francis, the Holy Land, the Bible and your spiritual life will have been immeasurably enriched and will never again be the same.

The Stones Cry Out is a treasure trove of insights and inspiration that belongs on the bookshelf of every Christian and every student of the Bible. The reader will come away with a greater appreciation for not only the land of the Lord but the Lord of the land.

Henry Gariepy

Preface

While God's consummate Word is complete and effectual in itself, an understanding of the geography, history and social context of biblical times is of immeasurable benefit to the student of the Word. With this in mind, some have referred to the Land of Israel (*Eretz Israel*) as "the *Fifth* Gospel."

All who take the Bible seriously want to know more about the wonderful reality and truths it contains. Over the centuries, biblical places and characters have assumed an almost fabled understanding. Yet Capernaum, the Jordan River, Jerusalem and the Sea of Galilee are not mythical names. They are real places. And David, Peter and Jesus are real people who lived in these places.

We have traveled to Israel, Jordan and Egypt on nine occasions both as tour hosts and on personal visits. Each sojourn has been like opening the Bible for the first time. It is fresh; it is enlightening; it is inspiring; it is the journey of a lifetime. One fellow traveler described his pilgrimage as seeing the Bible in three-dimension for the first time. Another likened the experience to seeing the Bible "in color" after reading it in black and white for so many years.

While we have had the estimable joy of introducing hundreds of people to *Eretz Israel*, my ardent prayer is that those who will not travel there in this life will, in some measure, vicariously relish the experience through these pages.

With respect to the content of the book, my primary purpose has been to provide brief introductory information on eighteen major locations which Jesus frequented during his earthly ministry. The chief criterion for including a site is its authenticity as established by conventional scholarship.

My method has been to furnish a brief overview of the geography, history, archaeological findings and spiritual significance of each site. The treatment is conspicuously limited. It is my hope that the succinct introduction and reflection on each location will wet the reader's appetite for further exploration through biblical research and, if possible, by taking a personal pilgrimage to the Holy Land.

My use of the term "Holy Land" throughout the book is not intended to ignore modern political realities but to facilitate an over-view of the geography and history through the ages. The expression "Holy Land" in this book refers to that portion of the eastern Mediter-ranean seaboard south of the Lebanon and Anti-Lebanon Mountains, with the Mediterranean Sea as the western boundary, the Arabian Desert as the eastern boundary and the Sinai Desert as the southern boundary. Using present-day political borders, the Holy Land in-cludes the modern State of Israel, the Hashemite Kingdom of Jordan and the so-called occupied territories of the Gaza Strip, West Bank and Golan Heights now under Israeli control.

Now , with the Prophet Isaiah I entreat you to "'. . . Come, let us go up to the mountain of the Lord, to the house of the God of Jacob. He will teach us his ways, so that we may walk in his paths.' The law will go out from Zion, the word of the Lord from Jerusalem" (Isaiah 2:3).

William W. Francis
Suffern, New York
January 1993

Bethlehem

Sheep grazing in the Shepherds' Field. In the background is the Greek Orthodox Church erected near the traditional site of the Grotto of the Shepherds.

A GREETING TO BETHLEHEM

FROM ZION I GREET THEE, BETHLEHEM,
IN THE DAUGHTER I SEE THEE, THE MOTHER.

IN YOU A GUIDING STAR LIT UP,
AND IN THIS CITY A MULTITUDE OF FIERY TONGUES.

THE STAR GUIDED THE MAGI,
THE TONGUES ILLUMINATED PARTHIANS AND MEDES
AND ALL OTHER NATIONS WITH THEIR REDEEMING LIGHT.

THROUGH YOU THE BREAD WAS LEAVENED,
BUT ZION PREPARED THE MEAL.

YOUR MANGER NOURISHED THE LAMB,
BUT ZION LED IT TO THE ALTAR.

YOU WRAPPED JESUS IN SWADDLING CLOTHES,
BUT IN ZION HE BARED TO THOMAS HIS BREAST.

YOU SHELTERED THE VIRGIN WOMB
WHICH CONCEIVED, YET KNEW NO MAN,
BUT HERE IS A BRIDAL CHAMBER,
WHICH ADMITTED THE GROOM THROUGH LOCKED DOORS.

—Hesichios

Hesichios, a priest in Jerusalem, composed this ode to Bethlehem in the year 420 A.D. Through these brief lines the poet-priest echoes the close link between Jerusalem (Zion) and Bethlehem.

*B*ETHLEHEM — the very name floods the imagination and stirs the emotions. God chose this tiny village, annually revered in churches and homes around the world, as the cradle of celestial joy, hope and peace. Each Christmas young and old contemplate the reality and significance of the manger, the shepherds, the Magi and the Holy Family under the star of Bethlehem. In this hamlet one quiet, mysterious night two thousand years ago, an event took place that forever changed the course of history!

Modern Bethlehem, a modest village of 30,000 inhabitants (mostly Christian Arabs), is remarkably unchanged since the time of Jesus' birth. Perched on the rugged slopes of the Judean Desert five miles south of Jerusalem, Bethlehem sits along the main highway to Hebron and Egypt, known as "the Way of the Patriarchs." Its Hebrew name *Beth-Lehem* ("House of Bread") well defines this fertile parcel of land on the edge of the Judean desert. As they have through the ages, Bethlehem's fields still supply nourishing grain; the olive grove's distinctive oil; and the vineyard's succulent grapes.

Archaeologists have not excavated the site of ancient Bethlehem, located near the Church of the Nativity. No one knows when the village was first occupied. Called Ephrath ("fruitful") in Jacob's time, it became the burial place for his beloved wife, Rachel. Following the

The entrance to the Church of the Nativity is known as the "Door of Humility" since all who enter must bend their head and knees. The pointed arch dates from Crusader times. During the Ottoman period it was partially walled up to prevent mounted horsemen from entering the church.

A view of Bethlehem from the east near the Shepherds' Field.

Bethlehem

3

The Church of the Nativity viewed from Manger Square. The grotto where Jesus was born is directly below the small white cross on top of the church in the center of the picture.

Bottom left: The Herodium, a fortress built by Herod the Great on top of a steep, isolated mountain at the edge of the Judean Wilderness, dominates Bethlehem's southeast horizon. According to Josephus Flavius, Herod was buried here, but excavations have not yet revealed a tomb.

Bottom right: A donkey pauses for nourishment in the Shepherds' Field with Bethlehem on the horizon.

conquest of Canaan, the Israelites called it Bethlehem. According to 1 Chronicles 2:51, Salma, one of Caleb's sons, was the "Father of Bethlehem." It also was the home of Ibzan, the tenth judge; Elimelech, father-in-law of Ruth, as well as her husband, Boaz.

The Prophet Samuel established the town's religious significance. He came to Bethlehem declaring, ". . . I have come to sacrifice to the Lord. Consecrate yourselves and come to the sacrifice with me" (1 Samuel 16:5). Participants in that sacrifice — Jesse and his sons, along with their descendants — have immortalized Bethlehem. A thousand years after King David was born, his teenage progeny, Mary, gave birth to the King of Kings in their ancestral home, ". . . the city of David, which is called Bethlehem" (Luke 2:4, KJV).

At the time of Jesus' birth, shepherds were keeping watch over their sheep in a nearby field, and "an angel of the Lord appeared to them. . ." (Luke 2:9). While no one knows the exact spot where the angel appeared to the startled shepherds, tradition identifies two sites.

Bethlehem

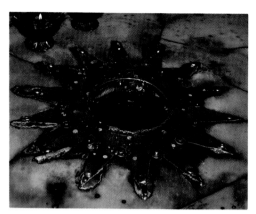

Preceding page, above and right: The Grotto of the Nativity's focal point is the fourteen-point silver star marking the place of Jesus' birth. The inscription reads "Hic de Virgine Maria Jesus Christus natus est" — "Here Jesus Christ was born to the Virgin Mary."

Both lie on the outskirts of the Christian-Arab village of Bet Shaur, now an eastern suburb of the town of Bethlehem. One of the sites, known locally as Deir el-Ranat ("Convent of the Shepherds") is also identified with the biblical Tower of Edar where Jacob sojourned after Rachel's death (Genesis 35:21). Excavations in 1972 showed that fourth century Christians revered the site. Generally, sites identified before the fifth century A.D. are strong evidence of authenticity.

Further to the east of Bet Shaur is a plain known as the Field of Ruth. In these pastoral surroundings, Ruth the Moabitess met and fell in love with Boaz (Ruth 2).

In the second century, Justin Martyr wrote that Jesus' birth took place "in a cave close to the village." The probability that this cave is identical to the grotto of the Church of the Nativity is supported by one of history's ironies. The identification and location of many Christian holy sites are owed to a pagan Roman emperor!

The Emperor Hadrian desecrated the Cave of the Nativity following the bloody repression of the Bar Kokhba revolt in 135 A.D. He encompassed the cave with a temple dedicated to the Roman god, Adonis, lover of Venus. Ironically, this desecration served to pinpoint the site forever.

Even before the Emperor Constantine laid the foundation of the Church of the Nativity in 326 A.D., Christians were making pilgrimages to the pagan temple. In 315 A.D. Eusebius wrote, "Up till the present day the local population of Bethlehem bears witness to the ancestral tradition and proceeds to show visitors the grotto in which the Virgin gave birth to the Child."

At the urging of his devout mother, Queen Helena, the Emperor Constantine removed Hadrian's Temple and found the grotto intact. He then built a magnificent basilica over the site, richly decorating it with marble mosaics and frescoes. What had been a simple cave at the edge of an obscure village became the "heart" of the town of Bethlehem and the focal point of Christian thought and devotion throughout the world.

Eventually, Constantine's basilica deteriorated. In the sixth century, the Emperor Justinian initiated an ambitious rebuilding program. The old church was demolished; its floor covered with 20 inches of soil and the new church erected on a higher level. Excavators have uncovered a small portion of the fourth century tile floor. Through an opening cut in the center of the church's nave, one can view this exquisite floor.

The Church of the Nativity today is basically the Justinian basilica; little has changed. Descending into the grotto under the central altar, one follows a well-worn path. Numberless pilgrims have entered this cave believed to be the authentic site of Jesus' birth.

The grotto's focal point is a fourteen-point silver star on the white marble floor. The star bears the Latin inscription "Hic de Virgine Maria Jesus Christus natus est" (Here Jesus Christ was born to the Virgin Mary).

In the north side of the cave is a marble-faced trough indicating where Mary laid Jesus. Facing the manger is an altar dedicated to the Wise Men. Many oil lamps illuminate the grotto. Fireproof material now covers the cave's walls, a precaution against fires that have caused serious damage in the past.

Here, in a hostel's basement cave in the village known as "The House of Bread," was born the baby who would one day declare — "I am the bread of life. . . I am the living bread that came down from heaven. If anyone eats of this bread, he will live forever. This bread is my flesh, which I will give for the life of the world" (John 6:48, 51).

May the Babe of Bethlehem's followers continue to respond as did his first century disciples — "Lord, evermore give us this bread" (John 6:34, KJV).

An old road sign points the way to the Cave of the Nativity.

Above: In a shallow cavity of the grotto a manger (right) carved from stone afforded the infant Jesus his first crib. The Altar of the Magi (left) faces the manger.

Left: An Arab home in Bethany makes use of natural caves as did first century inhabitants of Israel. The cave to the left is used as a stable. In the year 4 B.C., near an overcrowded Bethlehem inn, a similar stable provided emergency shelter for Joseph, Mary and their newborn son.

Nazareth

Modern Nazareth is an important stop for Christian pilgrims. The gray pyramidal dome of the magnificent Church of the Annunciation dominates the town center (left center).

While Bethlehem may have been "small among the clans of Judah" (Micah 5:2), Nazareth was an even smaller village of little significance. The Old Testament does not mention it. Despite its later fame, Nazareth was a place of ridicule in Jesus' day. Nathaniel echoed the widely held opinion when he quipped, "Nazareth! Can anything good come from there?" (John 1:46).

In both Arabic and Hebrew, Nazareth means "guardian," perhaps referring to the town's strategic location halfway between the Sea of Galilee and the Mediterranean Sea. The town lies on the western and northwestern slopes of a hollow among the lower hills of Galilee, just before they plunge into the Jezreel Valley (Valley of Esdraelon). Although excavations under the Church of the Annunciation indicate that the site has been settled since the Middle Bronze Age (2200-1500 B.C.), the village did not achieve recognition until Jesus' time.

Jesus' boyhood town was disdained, and its later inhabitants were contemptuously called *nasara* ("Christians"). Both the Roman and Arab neighbors periodically attacked Nazareth. When the conquering Crusaders arrived in 1099, Nazareth became a bishopric and the administrative center of Galilee. The Mamlukes succeeded in decimating the town in 1263. Nazareth endured 400 years of abandonment until the Franciscans resettled the town in the 17th century.

In this obscure Galilean village Mary received the Annunciation from the angel Gabriel (Luke 1:26-38); Joseph welcomed some celestial reassurance (Matthew 1:18-21) and *Y'shua* ("Jesus") grew to manhood (Luke 2:51-52). Jesus began his ministry in Nazareth. From his hometown he traveled to nearby towns and villages to preach and teach (Matthew 2:23, 4:13; Mark 1:9). Nazareth has consequently become one of the most holy sites in all Christendom, holding comparable status with Bethlehem and Jerusalem.

When Jesus was a boy, Nazareth was a small, quiet hamlet. Today, it is the largest Arab town in Galilee, providing administrative services for the surrounding towns. Its present population of over 30,000 contains a diverse ethnic and religious population. Moslem Arabs and Jews make up about two-thirds of the population. The remaining third includes Christian Arabs, along with Catholic, Greek Orthodox and Maronite Christian communities.

The largest church in Nazareth is the Church of the Annunciation —one of the most lavishly decorated churches in all Israel. According to an early Christian tradition, the church is built over the site of the house of Mary and Joseph, where the angel told Mary that she would "give birth to a son, and . . . give him the name Jesus" (Luke 1:31).

Other traditional sites in Nazareth include the Church of St. Joseph, presumably built over its namesake's carpentry shop; the Church of the Rock, where Jesus and his disciples allegedly dined after the resurrection, and the Church Synagogue, where Jesus preached and antagonized the Nazarene community (Luke 4:14-30). While these sites commemorate a location or event, the only site that has some claim to authenticity is the spring near the Church of Gabriel, which is built over the Fountain of Mary.

Until recently, a fountain on the northern outskirts of downtown Nazareth furnished an abundant water supply from the nearby spring. Since this is the only natural spring in Nazareth, it is likely that Jesus came here as a child with his mother. The water of the Fountain of

Except for the village spring, none of the places in Nazareth associated by tradition with the events in the life of Mary, Joseph and Jesus can be verified. Everyone in Nazareth, including the Holy Family, would have used the sole spring. The Church of Saint Gabriel marks the source of this spring.

The steep precipice known as the Mount of the Leap ("Har Kedumin") plunges from Nazareth to the Jezreel Valley. According to the biblical record, the townsmen took Jesus to ". . . the brow of the hill on which the town was built, in order to throw him down the cliff. But he walked right through the crowd and went on his way" (Luke 4:29-30).

Road signs point the way to Nazareth.

Bottom left: A Greek Orthodox priest leads a funeral procession from the Church of Saint Gabriel.

Bottom right: The crest of the Mount of the Leap offers a breathtaking panoramic view of the famed valley known by three names: Esdraelon, Jezreel and Armageddon.

Mary inside the Church of Gabriel, a Greek Orthodox Church built in 1769, flows into the sanctuary from this spring. From here the water was piped to the public fountain outside.

Archaeologists have uncovered a significant artifact called the Nazareth Decree. The inscription tablet was an *Ordinance of Caesar*, declaring it a crime to violate or rob sealed graves. Some scholars have suggested that the "tomb robbers' inscription" is one reason for the sealing of Christ's tomb and the stationing of Roman guards at the entrance. It was apparently a general decree meant to control the notorious practice of grave-robbing.

Luke records the startling events of the memorable *Shabbot* ("Sabbath") in the synagogue of Nazareth (Luke 4:14-30). Jesus returned "in the power of the Spirit" to his home town. News of his ministry had spread throughout the land, and his popularity was reaching its zenith. As was his custom, Jesus entered the synagogue on the Sabbath. He stood to read from the scriptures and requested the scroll of the prophet Isaiah. Unrolling the scroll to the 61st chapter, he read:

> *The Spirit of the Lord is on me, because he has anointed me to preach good news to the poor. He has sent me to proclaim freedom for the prisoners and recovery of sight for the blind, to release the oppressed, to proclaim the year of the Lord's favor.*   — Luke 4:18-19

Handing the scroll back to the attendant, he sat down and declared:

> *Today this scripture is fulfilled in your hearing.*   — Luke 4:21

Jesus declared both his mission and ministry by applying Isaiah's messianic prophecy to himself. This act of apparent blasphemy enraged the congregation. They grabbed Jesus, dragged him to the brow of a hill outside the village and tried to throw him off.

According to the biblical record, they took him to "the brow of the hill on which the town was built" (Luke 4:29). The only area matching this description is an awe-inspiring, steep precipice on the south side of the village known as the Mount of the Leap ("Har Kedumin"). Although the

Bible says ". . . he walked right through the crowd and went on his way" (Luke 4:30), a tradition developed that he leaped from the mountain.

The crest of the Mount of the Leap offers a breathtaking panoramic view of the famed valley known by three names: Esdraelon, Jezreel, Armageddon. Bible stories spring to life as modern pilgrims scan the east-west horizon. To the far east looms the dome-shaped Mount Tabor, where the prophetess Deborah and Barak defeated King Jabin's army, commanded by Sisera (Judges 4). To the south the villages of Endor (1 Samuel 28) and Nain (Luke 7:11-17), nestled in the protecting ridges of the Hill Moreh (Judges 7), are clearly visible. The imposing Mount Gilboa, site of King Saul and his sons' demise (1 Samuel 31), defines the horizon behind the Hill Moreh. On a clear day the tell of Megiddo, Solomon's fortified chariot city (1 Kings 9:15-19), is visible, as well as the 13-mile long Mount Carmel (1 Kings 18:16-46) to the west.

Jesus knew these landmarks well. Although insignificant and disdained in his day, Jesus' boyhood home provided a biblical panorama unparalleled in all Israel — a backdrop which one day will set the stage for the catastrophic events preceding his millennial reign. Nazareth will witness the momentous events vividly described by John in The Revelation. Before the final outpouring of God's wrath, the kings of the earth will gather for the last battle in "the place that in Hebrew is called Armageddon" (Revelation 16:16).

Scenes from Nazareth's open market are as common today as 2000 years ago. Mondays and Thursdays were market days in Nazareth, as they were throughout the country. Mary would have joined the women of Nazareth in the open-air market to buy produce from traveling peddlers.

Jordan River

The only major river in Israel, the Jordan has always played an important historic and symbolic role.

From its three principle sources in the foothills of snowcapped Mount Hermon, the Jordan River meanders its way 80 miles due south to the Dead Sea. Its tortuous zigzag route, however, stretches the largest river in Israel to about 200 miles. En route it flows through the marshy Huleh Valley into the Sea of Galilee, continuing through the Jordan Valley to the Dead Sea. The entire span is part of the Syro-African rift, a vast geological fault in the earth's crust.

A rapid descent marks the river's course. Melting snow from Mount Hermon's peak (9,232 feet above sea level) cascades through numerous shallow tributaries, merging near Kibbutz Sede Nehemiah to form the Jordan River. In all, the Jordan plummets about 3,000 feet over its 80-mile journey south. From 1700 feet above sea level at its inception, the river drops to 680 feet below sea level upon entering the Sea of Galilee. Eventually it descends to 1300 feet below sea level when it reaches the Dead Sea, the lowest spot on earth.

Although the Jordan (*Yarden* in Hebrew) is neither deep nor wide, it is the best-known river in the world. From Lot's choice of the well-watered plain of Jordan (Genesis 13:10) to Jesus' final crossing of the Jordan before his crucifixion (John 10:40), the Jordan River serves

The Stones Cry Out

as landmark and backdrop to numerous biblical events.

Joshua led the Israelites across the Jordan into the promised land (Joshua 3-4). David fled across the Jordan from his rebellious son, Absalom (2 Samuel 17:24-26). Naaman the leper obeyed the Prophet Elisha's instruction. "So he went down and dipped himself in the Jordan seven times . . . and his flesh was restored and became clean like that of a young boy" (2 Kings 5:14). John heralded the beginning of Jesus' earthly ministry by baptizing God's "beloved Son" in the Jordan River (Matthew 3:13-17).

In first century Palestine the safest and easiest (although not shortest) route from Galilee to Jerusalem was along the Jordan River's eastern bank. This well-traveled road crossed the river south of the Sea of Galilee and continued south through the land of Perea. Today, this route passes through the Hashemite Kingdom of Jordan. Since the Jordan River is the boundary between Israel and Jordan, traveling the ancient route is not a viable option for tourists today. One look at the flat eastern bank, however, will explain why Jesus often came "into the coasts of Judaea by the farther side of Jordan" (Mark 10:1, KJV) instead of taking the shorter, but exhausting, undulating road on the western bank.

The exact site of Jesus' baptism is not clear. John says it took place in "Bethany on the other side of the Jordan" (John 1:28). Although not identified, Christian tradition since at least the sixth century points to the Hajlah Ford east of Jericho. This area now lies in the demilitarized zone between Israel and Jordan. Today, no one can visit the site due to current political tensions.

The Monastery of John the Baptist that commemorates the site can nevertheless be seen from the road leading to the Dead Sea just south of Jericho. The monastery's medieval structure encloses the remains of a fifth century Byzantine church destroyed by the invading Persians

The Jordan River is neither deep nor wide. It varies from three to ten feet (one to three meters) in depth and is up to 90 feet (30 meters) wide.

The Monastery of John the Baptist (extreme left), commemorating the site of Jesus' baptism, can be seen in the distance from the road leading to the Dead Sea just south of Jericho. The hills of Moab (located in the Kingdom of Jordan) outline the distant horizon.

In the cold, shallow water near the river's bank, John the Baptist heralded the beginning of Jesus' earthly ministry by baptizing God's "beloved Son" (Matthew 3:13-17).

in 614 A.D. and rebuilt in 1128. The edifice was renovated in 1954 and since 1967 has been within the military zone separating Israel and Jordan. Only two monks now care for the monastery.

Not far from this site, the Children of Israel crossed the Jordan River into the Promised Land. The Bible vividly describes this pivotal event in history:

> *The water from upstream stopped flowing. It piled up in a heap a great distance away, at a town called Adam in the vicinity of Zarethan, while the water flowing down to the Sea of the Arabah (the Salt Sea) was completely cut off. So the people crossed over opposite Jericho.*
> — Joshua 3:16

Twelve centuries after this historic milestone, and following four hundred years of prophetic silence, John the Baptist launched an unprecedented spiritual revival ". . . in the desert. He went into all the country around the Jordan, preaching a baptism of repentance for the forgiveness of sins" (Luke 3:2-3). People flocked to hear this curious character clothed in camel's hair preaching repentance and the coming of the long-awaited Messiah. Those who accepted his message and confessed their sins, ". . . were baptized by him in the Jordan River" (Matthew 3:6). The Apostle John precisely notes that "this all happened at Bethany on the other side of the Jordan. . ." (John 1:28).

Baptism was a vivid illustration of the transformed life. John's audience understood well the concept of baptism. It was only through a baptismal rite that a proselyte came into Judaism from another faith. The crowd readily grasped the idea that baptism represented a death to the old and a rebirth to the new. The day before Jesus' baptism, John chastised the priests and Levites, and he explicitly denied being the Christ (John 1:19-27). In the meantime, Jesus arrived from Galilee and startled his cousin by coming to the water's edge "to be baptized by John" (Matthew 3:13). As with Peter in the Upper Room (John 13:1-9), John at first attempted to reverse the roles Jesus had required. John wanted Jesus to baptize him. Jesus responded as he later would with Peter, insisting that John explicitly follow his command. John obeyed. As soon as Jesus came out of the Jordan, God's divine imprimatur arrived in the form of a dove. A voice from heaven declared, "This is my Son, whom I love; with him I am well pleased" (Matthew 3:17).

What a remarkable event. A rare, divine moment when all three persons of the Trinity were simultaneously and tangibly operative. The Son submitted, the Holy Spirit descended, the Father spoke.

Jesus did not need to repent and receive forgiveness of sin. Nevertheless, he insisted that John baptize him as a symbol that the new covenant was about to fulfill and replace the old. Never before John's preaching had a Jew submitted himself to baptism; the ritual was strictly reserved for proselytes. "Let it be so now;" Jesus said, "it is proper for us to do this to fulfill all righteousness" (Matthew 3:15).

Immediately after Jesus' baptism ". . . the Spirit sent him out into

A herd of goats graze on the slopes of Mount Hermon. Called the "Mountain of the Old Man" (Jabel-esh-Sheikh) by the Arabs, Mount hermon lifts its white, dignified head 9,232 feet above the level of the Mediterranean Sea to the west. Melting snow from Mount Hermon's peak flows through numerous shallow tributaries, merging near Kibbutz Sede Nehemiah to form the Jordan River.

Jordan River

the desert, and he was in the desert forty days, being tempted by Satan. He was with the wild animals, and angels attended him" (Mark 1:12-13). The same Spirit who came upon him at his baptism, now sent him across the Jordan into the nearby desert to be tested.

Jesus would cross the Jordan River numerous times before the sudden death of his friend Lazarus required that he cross the Jordan for the last time (John 11). Only the Apostle John records his last visit to the Jordan:

> *Then Jesus went back across the Jordan to the place where John had been baptizing in the early days. Here he stayed and many people came to him. They said, "Though John never performed a miraculous sign, all that John said about this man was true." And in that place many believed in Jesus.* — John 10:40-42

Geographically, the unimpressive, meandering Jordan River may well be characterized as the least among the rivers of the world. Nevertheless, in terms of biblical history and theology it is elevated to eminent prominence. Indeed, it is the river above all others. Transcending even its historic significance, the Jordan River is a celebrated metaphor of the Christian life. As it issues from Mount Hermon and flows through the Sea of Galilee, the Jordan represents the exhilarating, dedicated life outpoured in service for Christ. It is full of life; healthy. On the other hand, its terminus, the Dead Sea, is stagnant, lifeless, having no outlet. So too, the Christian without an outlet for faith becomes self-centered, spiritually stagnant and lifeless.

The Jordan River also represents the divine invitation to every believer to "cross over" into the fullness and joy of life in the Spirit. As Moses reminded the Children of Israel, these "are not just idle words for you — they are your life. By them you will live long in the land you are crossing the Jordan to possess" (Deuteronomy 32:47).

At its southern extremity, the Sea of Galilee constricts to continue the Jordan River's flow south. From this point to where the river joins the Dead Sea is only 70 miles (110 kilometers); yet constant meandering lengthens its shoreline to 200 miles (320 kilometers).

The Stones Cry Out

Sea of Galilee

Modern pilgrims return to Tiberias after a memorable day on the Sea of Galilee.

Every morning, rain or shine, the Sea of Galilee hosts an ecumenical flotilla of tourists. An aura of excitement and anticipation permeates the atmosphere as wayfarers from around the world eagerly board the specially-crafted skiffs docked in Tiberias. Each traveler senses that this will be the excursion of a lifetime — until this moment, a voyage that was but a dream. For many pilgrims, the boat ride from Tiberias to Capernaum becomes the catalyst transforming a conventional tour into an extraordinary pilgrimage. The journey on this lake Jesus knew so well redefines the phrase "unforgettable experience."

Nearing the lake's center, the captain cuts the engine. The resulting silence acknowledges the compelling need for serene reflection in the midst of these sacred, tranquil surroundings. The faint, muted sounds of familiar hymns and choruses soon fill the air as each aquatic congregation seeks to verbalize the awe and wonder of this memorable moment.

Following a time of singing, meditation and prayer, the passengers reluctantly weigh anchor and proceed to the northern shore. They dock near the ruins of the town Jesus chose as headquarters during his public ministry — Capernaum.

Located some sixty miles north of Jerusalem, the Sea of Galilee remains the main source of fresh water in a country that is 60% desert. To say that the Sea of Galilee is the lifeblood of this country, where natural resources are scarce, goes beyond metaphor.

The surface of the Sea of Galilee covers 66 square miles and is 685 feet below the level of the Mediterranean Sea. Its depth varies up to

Crusader ruins (lower center) still stand at the water's edge in Teberias. The imposing Golan Heights, annexed by Israel in 1981, towers above the Sea of Galilee on the opposite eastern shore.

150 feet. The Jordan River plunges south from Mount Hermon, entering the Sea of Galilee at its northern end (near ancient Bethsaida) and flows out the southern end, a distance of about thirteen miles. The lake's greatest width is eight miles at Magdala.

Of the nine towns surrounding the lake in Jesus' day, only Magdala (Migdal) and Tiberias remain. The other seven communities have all but vanished. Only fragmentary vestiges remain of these neighborhoods that once thrived on the fishing trade. The Gospel accounts depict fishing as a prosperous industry. Today, however, relatively few boats have replaced the fleets of fishing vessels found in biblical times.

Although Migdal endures as a modest village, Tiberias is the sole surviving community that fits the definition of a city. Located on Galilee's western shore, Tiberias dates its founding to 18-22 A.D. Herod Antipas built this splendid resort city in honor of the Roman emperor, Tiberius. By the time the city was completed, a young 26-year-old rabbi from Nazareth was preparing for his approaching public ministry.

Built by the despised Romans, Tiberias was host to few Jews. In addition, there persisted a widely spread false rumor that Tiberias was built over a cemetery. This made it "unclean," according to the

The New Testament town of Gergesa set on the eastern shore between the two hills cutting into the Golan Heights (center). The precipice to the right of Gergesa is likely where the swine were herded headlong into the sea by demons Jesus cast out of a madman called Legion.

Shabtai "Shep" Levanon, a popular Israeli guide, pauses in the midst of the Sea of Galilee to impart important background information before a time of meditation and singing.

Jewish religious leaders. As a matter of principle and religious dogma Jews avoided this pagan testimonial to Roman domination. For these reasons, it is unlikely that Jesus ever set foot in Tiberias.

Tiberias today is a fascinating, lively and affable Israeli resort community. The warm temperate climate and hot mineral springs have attracted tourists since Roman times. For two millennia people have used the hot springs of Tiberias to treat various illnesses, especially rheumatism and respiratory diseases. Tiberias endures as a thriving tourist resort with numerous modern hotels catering to Christian pilgrims and Israeli vacationers.

The Old Testament refers to the lake as Yam Kinneret ("the Sea of Kinneret"). *Kinneret*, a Hebrew word meaning "harp-shaped," accurately describes the shoreline's contour that resembles an ancient lyre or *kinnor* (Genesis 4:21). Throughout the Old Testament, writers frequently mention Yam Kinneret with the borders of the land inhabited by the twelve tribes (Numbers 34:11, Deuteronomy 3:17, Joshua 13:27).

Luke called the Sea of Galilee "the Lake of Gennesaret" (Luke 5:1). He described it as the center of a thriving fishing industry in New Testament times. Nine busy and prosperous cities surrounded the

Tiberias, the magnificent capital of New Testament Galilee, was built by Herod Antipas (who killed John the Baptist) between the years 18-22 A.D. on the western shore of the Sea of Galilee. Named in honor of the reigning Roman Emperor, Tiberias became known throughout the Roman world for its splendid palace, forum, public baths and hot springs.

The Stones Cry Out

Fishermen carry on their time honored profession in much the same way as their Galilean ancestors.

lake, each having a population of not less than 15,000 inhabitants. The entire seaside population exceeded 150,000!

Jesus spent most of his public life around the Sea of Galilee. Throughout the lake region Jesus preached about the kingdom of God. Walking the shoreline between Tabgha and Capernaum, Jesus called his first disciples, four of whom were fishermen, and commissioned them as fishers of men (Luke 5:1-11). In Capernaum and environs he delivered the majority of his teachings. He performed over one-third of his recorded miracles around or on the Sea of Galilee.

Jesus crossed this celebrated sea on several occasions. He visited the towns and villages around the lake, at times retreating into the surrounding hills alone to pray. While the water is pure and usually calm, sudden storms can turn the tranquil lake into raging currents with high waves. Cold air sweeping through the Huleh Valley from Mount Hermon spawns fierce and furious storms when it converges with warm air rising from the lake. Jesus rebuked just such a storm (Mark 4:39), and on one occasion, he walked on the tempestuous water (Matthew 14:22-34).

The contemporary pilgrim can indeed walk and sail in the Master's steps around and across the Sea of Galilee. Surrounded by the inexplicable beauty and serenity of this picturesque setting, those who "have ears to hear" (Luke 14:35) will perceive afresh the sublime, universal invitation from the Man of Galilee — "Come, follow me . . . and I will make you fishers of men" (Matthew 4:19).

Water from the Sea of Galilee is pumped to all parts of Israel. Some of this crystalline water ends in the Negev bringing to fulfillment the prophecy ". . . the desert shall rejoice, and the blossom as the rose" (Isaiah 35:1).

Capernaum

N estled among a cluster of eucalyptus and palm trees on the northwestern shore of the Sea of Galilee lie the ruins of the once-prestigious city of Capernaum. Today, only the lofty Corinthian pillars of the white marble third century synagogue endure — mute testimony to the city's past glory. The sound of gentle breezes whispering through palm trees and deep purple bougainvillea bushes has replaced the stir and excitement of two millennia ago.

In Jesus' day, this bustling metropolis was the largest and wealthiest city along the shores of the lake and in all Galilee. A mixed race of Jews and Gentiles has inhabited Galilee (the northern part of Naphtali) since Old Testament times (Judges 1:33). The prophet Isaiah called it "Galilee of the Gentiles" (NIV) or "Galilee of the nations" (Isaiah 9:1, KJV). Thriving on the steady economy provided by the fishing trade, the diverse population of Greeks, Romans and Jews had learned to live at peace and mutual respect.

The city's prestige did not rely solely on its booming economy. Capernaum was a political center, housing the office of a tax collector (Mark 2:14) and the residence of a high officer of King Herod Antipas (Matthew 8:5-13, Luke 7:1-10). Herod Antipas was the son of Herod the Great and Tetrarch of Galilee and Perea. Along with Tiberias, its

Capernaum as viewed from the Mount of Beatitudes. The ruins of the ancient city are camouflaged by a cluster of eucalyptus trees (center) on the northern shore of the Sea of Galilee.

The Stones Cry Out

sister city on the lake, Capernaum strongly influenced the economy and politics of first century Galilee.

Above left: This menorah carved in stone was found in the synagogue's ruins.

To reach Capernaum, Jesus walked a day's journey from his home in Nazareth, through the expansive Valley of the Doves and past the imposing cliffs at Arbel. Pausing for refreshment in Magdala, Jesus met Mary Magdalene from whom he cast out seven devils (Luke 8:2). A short three-mile journey to the north brought him to the city he chose as the center of his activities for the last two years of his life. Capernaum became Jesus' headquarters, "his own town," according to Matthew 9:1.

Above right: Carving of a synagogue on wheels, symbolizing that it is a temporary substitution for the Temple in Jerusalem.

Capernaum was also the home of Peter (Luke 4:38) and is the place where Jesus often taught in the synagogue (Mark 1:21). Here Jesus manifested his goodness and power. His Capernaum miracles include the healing of the centurion's palsied servant (Matthew 8:5-13), the paralytic who was lowered through a roof by four friends (Mark 2:1-12) and a nobleman's son (John 4:46-54).

Standing at the gate of Capernaum's excavated ruins are the author's wife and daughter.

Jesus' presence made Capernaum a city of miracles! Of the thirty-five recorded miracles Jesus performed, twelve took place in Capernaum and ten more in nearby towns or on the Sea of Galilee. Two-thirds of his recorded miraculous signs took place in or around Capernaum!

Despite Jesus' remarkable miracles and revolutionary teaching, the people of Capernaum did not repent. Jesus pronounced a curse upon the city for their indifference — "And you, Capernaum, will you be exalted to heaven? You shall be brought down to Hades. For if the mighty works done in you had been done in Sodom, it would have remained until this day. But I tell you that it shall be more tolerable on the day of judgment for the land of Sodom than for you" (Matthew 11:23-24, RSV).

The prophecy concerning this ungrateful city has been fulfilled. Capernaum was destroyed and the site lost for centuries. The

The ornate top of a marble column that once supported the synagogue's balcony where devout women would come for worship. The Church of the Beatitudes can be seen (far left) in the distance.

archaeological site of Kafar Naum is today little more than a meager assortment of ruins reflecting only a remnant of the city's former glory.

The first excavation in 1905 revealed Capernaum's most important edifice — the well-known third century synagogue. The distinguished biblical archaeologist and Middle East scholar, Dr. William F. Albright, confirms that it sets on the site of the first century synagogue. The Roman centurion whose servant Jesus healed erected this first synagogue. The third century structure incorporates numerous stones of the first synagogue. Stones still standing in this ancient synagogue once echoed with Jesus' voice as he worshiped, taught and performed miracles!

The citizens of Capernaum loved and respected the Roman centurion assigned to their city. Commanding a company of one hundred soldiers, he built a synagogue for the Jews. When the centurion's trusted servant was deathly sick, it was the Jewish elders who urged Jesus to heal him (Luke 7:3-5). Demonstrating genuine reverence for Jesus, he protested, "I do not deserve to have you come under my roof." Jesus responded with the amazing assertion, "I have not found anyone in Israel with such great faith." While another centurion, Cornelius, is correctly regarded as the first Gentile convert to post-

The Stones Cry Out

resurrection Christianity (Acts 10), it was the Roman centurion from Capernaum who first expressed faith in the Jewish Messiah.

Jesus seized this opportunity to teach the all-encompassing character of the Gospel. To the citizens of Capernaum Jesus said, " 'I say to you that many will come from the east and the west, and will take their places at the feast with Abraham, Isaac and Jacob in the kingdom of heaven'. . . Then Jesus said to the centurion, 'Go! It will be done just as you believed it would.' And his servant was healed at that very hour" (Matthew 8:11,13).

Though ancient Capernaum will forever remain a shattered ruin, the stones are not mute. They cry out the glorious truth that the Christ of Capernaum lives in triumph, forgiving and healing all who turn to him in faith.

Ruins of the third century synagogue. The white marble is contrasted by the first century foundations built of black basalt, common to the Galilee and Golan regions. The synagogue entrance (center) faces south toward Jerusalem.

Capernaum

Tabgha

A lone fisherman (center) tends to his nets in Tabgha.

A fifth century mosaic depicting a basket of bread and two fish at the Church of the Miracle of the Loaves and Fishes.

Less than half a mile south of Capernaum on the Sea of Galilee's northwestern shore is a small plain known today as Tabgha. The name *Tabgha* (or *Tavbha*) derives from the Arabic mispronunciation of the Greek word *Heptapegon,* meaning "seven springs." Its Hebrew name is *En Sheva.* As the name signifies, seven springs refresh Tabgha with a plentiful supply of hot mineral water from deep beneath the earth's surface.

The largest spring, Ein Nur, dispenses a steady flow of undrinkable, bluish, sulfuric water at a constant 81 degrees Farenheit. Ein Nur flows inside an enclosed pool next to the Tiberias-Rosh Pina road. The impressive octagonal pool of black basalt is built on Roman foundations. East of Ein Nur is a small fresh water spring known as Job's Spring. According to local tradition Job often washed in this spring.

The tepid mineral water mixing with the cool water of the lake has created a paradise for fish and fisherman since biblical times. As with their ancestors, fishermen still mend their nets in this tranquil spot on the lake shore.

This stretch of shoreline often bore the footprints of Jesus as he walked with his disciples, teaching and performing miracles on and near the water's edge. While the Bible rarely provides precise geographical details, this is likely the area familiar to the fishermen disciples — Peter, Andrew, James and John. Near these nutrient-saturated waters, Jesus invited Peter and Andrew to "Come, follow me, . . . and I will make you fishers of men" (Matthew 4:19).

In 1932 the archaeologists Mader and Schneider discovered the remains of a fourth century Byzantine church — The Church of the

Miracle of the Loaves and Fishes — in the area of Tabgha. The single-nave structure revealed some of the most striking and best preserved mosaics in Israel. A superb mosaic of birds, fishes, beasts and flowers form the church's floor. The well-known mosaic of a basket of loaves flanked by two fish lies beneath the altar.

The mosaics in the nave and north aisle contain simple geometric designs. In the five spaces between the columns are representations of various types of birds (geese, herons, etc.). The best preserved and most interesting mosaics, however, are in the north transept. The artist was obviously familiar with the Nile Delta since he depicted the flora and fauna of that area: flamingoes, herons, snakes and ducks among the lotus blossoms and reeds.

Tradition associates Tabgha with the site of the miracle of the loaves and fishes (Mark 6:30-44). John 6:1, however, clarifies the location of this miracle as taking place on the other side of the lake ("the far shore of the Sea of Galilee") near Peter and Philip's home-town of Bethsaida. This may be the reason Jesus asked the "hometown boy" Philip, "Where shall we buy bread for these people to eat?" (John 6:5).

Tabgha is best known as the site of Jesus' post-resurrection break-fast with his disciples as recorded by the beloved apostle (John 21). There is little doubt that the pebble strewn Tabgha shore witnessed the risen Lord's third appearance to his disciples.

Jesus often walked this stretch of shoreline from Capernaum to the seven springs of Tabgha. Along this expanse Jesus called his fishermen disciples and affirmed Peter's calling during the early morning post-resurrection breakfast recorded in the 21st chapter of John.

The Church of St. Peter, also known as the
Chapel of Primacy, in Tabgha.

Twentieth century fishermen follow in the
wake of their first century counterparts.

On Tabgha's beach Jesus prepared breakfast for his weary disciples returning from a fruitless night of fishing. The disciples no doubt enjoyed the fresh fish and warm bread "cooked to perfection" on a charcoal fire (John 21:9).

Surely, the setting reminded Peter of the recent night he stood around the only other charcoal fire mentioned in the New Testament. He no doubt remembered that inglorious night in the high priests' courtyard when ". . . the servants and officers stood there, who had made a fire of coals; for it was cold . . . and Peter stood with them, and warmed himself" (John 18:18, KJV). Around the high priests' fire he denied his Lord three times.

Jesus had prepared the setting and the agenda for Peter's psychological and spiritual healing. Paralleling Peter's threefold denial, Jesus asked three questions designed to teach Peter the meaning of selfless, *agape* love and commissioned him to "feed my sheep" (John 21:15-19).

The thrice-repeated question — "Do you love me?" — is far from redundant. Twice Jesus used the word for "complete, unselfish love" (*agape*). Each time Peter responded with the diminutive verb *phileo*, meaning "deep affection and respect." The third time, Jesus rephrased the question, poignantly using *phileo* instead of *agape* — "Simon son of John, do you love (*phileo*) me?" The modified question pierced Peter's heart. He could not profess the total love his Lord required. Not until Pentecost (Acts 2) did Peter understand the meaning of *agape* love.

The Chapel of Primacy (or Church of St. Peter) commemorates the risen Christ's seaside appearance to the apostles. In 1934 the Franciscans built a new structure over the remains of a fourth century church. They carefully constructed the Chapel of Primacy around a massive rock known since the Medieval Age as "Mensa Christi" — the Table of the Lord. Tradition marks this rock as the "table" where Jesus dined with his disciples. In the early fifth century, the Spanish pilgrim, Etheria, described the steps cut in the rock and continuing outside the church as "those on which the Lord stood."

Books and messages based on Jesus' dialogue with Peter abound. It is clear, however, that our Lord's primary intent was to lead Peter from the human to the divine level of loving commitment as a shepherd of his flock.

Unselfish affection, without the expectation of anything in return, must be the basic motivation for Christian service. Only as we strive to reflect the unadulterated, undiluted *agape* love of Christ can we genuinely tend and shepherd his sheep.

It is not coincidental that Jesus' final command to Peter (John 21:22) was identical to his initial call three years earlier (Matthew 4:19). First and last, Christ calls his disciples to obedience — "**Follow Me!**"

Statue commemorating the appearance of the risen Christ to the apostles on the shore of the Sea of Galilee when he commissioned Peter with the three-fold imperative — "Feed my lambs . . . Feed my sheep . . . Feed my sheep" (John 21:15-17).

One of Tabgha's seven hot mineral springs flows into the Sea of Galilee.

Mount of Beatitudes

Shoreline of Tabgha and the Mount of Beatitudes as viewed from the Sea of Galilee.

The Mount of Beatitudes rises above the ruins of Tabgha and Capernaum on the northwestern shore of the Sea of Galilee. This revered hill offers an awe-inspiring view of virtually the entire shoreline of the Sea of Galilee. From its summit one can readily identify the active communities of Tiberias and Migdal (Magdala), along with the ancient ruins of Capernaum and Gergesa.

The fifth-century pilgrim, Etheria, identified this hill as the place where Jesus did much of his preaching. The ruins of a fourth-century church known as the Monastery of the Sermon on the Mount are visible on the lower section of the hill, immediately north of the road to Capernaum near Tabgha.

A narrow access road branches from the Tiberias-Rosh Pina highway and leads up the hill to the stately Church of the Beatitudes and adjoining hospice, Ospizio Monte di Beatitudine. Built in 1936 by The Associazione Italiane, both facilities are now cared for by the Franciscan Sisters of the Immaculate Heart of Mary. The renowned architect

Antonio Barluzzi designed the distinctive octagonal-shaped church. He utilized the plentiful local basalt stone for the edifice and white stone from Nazareth (along with Roman travertine) to produce the unadorned, graceful arches surrounding the church's veranda.

Each of the sanctuary's eight walls commemorates (as the Latin inscriptions on the inside indicate) one of the Beatitudes pronounced at the beginning of the Sermon on the Mount (Matthew 5:3-10). A lofty, elegant central dome symbolizes the ninth Beatitude. It reminds every believer — Blessed (*happy*) are those who are persecuted because of righteousness, for theirs is the kingdom of heaven (Matthew 5:11-12).

It is the concave southeastern slope, however, that makes this hill one of the most hallowed Christian sites in the Holy Land. Since the fourth century, Christians have identified this verdant crest as the place where Jesus escaped the pressing multitude to teach his disciples. He retreated from the large crowds that had followed him from ". . . Galilee, the Decapolis, Jerusalem, Judea and the region across the Jordan. . ." (Matthew 4:25). The Master Rabbi led his disciples to this secluded natural amphitheater, sat down and taught them. His subsequent summary of basic Gospel themes is known as the Sermon on the Mount (Matthew 5-7).

As Matthew recounts the event — "Now when he saw the crowds, he went up on a mountainside and sat down. His disciples came to him, and he began to teach them, saying: 'Blessed are the poor in spirit, for theirs is the kingdom of heaven'" (Matthew 5:1-3). Since verses 3-11 begin with the words "Blessed are. . ." this section is

The Church of the Beatitudes crowns the summit of the hill rising above the ruins of Capernaum and Tabgha.

Mount of Beatitudes

known as the *Beatitudes*, which means "Blessing" in Latin.

It is important to note that on this occasion Jesus *sat down* to teach. When a Rabbi was formally teaching, or when the subject matter was of utmost importance, he sat down . Although rabbis routinely gave instruction while walking or standing, when it came time for formal, extensive teaching, the lecture was delivered while seated. The fact that Jesus sat down to teach his disciples indicates that what he was about to say was essential, fundamental and, in the paramount sense of the word, official.

The Mount of Beatitudes is also the traditional spot where Jesus chose his twelve disciples (Luke 6:12-16). Luke describes the solemn choosing of the Twelve — "One of those days Jesus went out to a mountainside to pray. . . When morning came, he called his disciples to him and chose twelve of them, whom he also designated apostles" (Luke 6:12-13). Apparently there were other followers present who were not chosen to be part of the inner circle of twelve. Jesus separated the twelve disciples and commissioned them as *apostles* ("one sent forth").

The Sermon on the Mount, according to Luke's narrative (Luke 6:17-49), immediately follows the choosing of the Twelve. While there are differences in Luke's and Matthew's reports, both start with a series of beatitudes, with clear parallels in the remaining content. Some believe the two records are different reports of the same sermon; others see it as substantially the same sermon delivered on separate occasions. Since Jesus was constantly teaching, it is likely that he expressed some of the same words and phrases in various forms hundreds of times. On this question, however, it is reasonable to conclude that both Matthew and Luke give a version of the Sermon on the Mount.

If, as Luke indicates, the Sermon on the Mount follows immediately the choosing of the Twelve, Jesus' forceful words take on added significance. The Master's instructions may best be understood as an

Below left: The Sea of Galilee's eastern shore as viewed from the Church of the Beatitudes.

Below right: A breathtaking view of the Sea of Galilee's western shoreline from the Mount of the Beatitudes. Jesus likely delivered the Sermon on the Mount from the natural amphitheater in the foreground. Magdala (modern Migdal), the town of "Mary who is called Magdalene" (Luke 8:2), is located in the dark green area where the shore turns sharply to the left. Tiberias is seen at the end of the shoreline in the upper left hand corner.

The Stones Cry Out

ordination address to the twelve apostles he had recently selected.

Whatever the context of this discourse, one thing is certain: Jesus here introduces and summarizes guidelines and instruction for life and ministry that are unique, unprecedented and revolutionary. The Sermon on the Mount is, in fact, a distillation of the whole Gospel message. Some have, therefore, more accurately referred to this treatise as "The Compendium of Christ's Doctrine" and "The Magna Carta of the Kingdom." Without question, the Sermon on the Mount contains the essence of Jesus' teaching to the inner circle of his chosen apostles.

Disciples from around the world pause on the Mount of Beatitudes to reflect on the essence of genuine, unfeigned discipleship. When they listen carefully for the voice of the Master (Matthew 11:15, Mark 4:9), they again hear him say — Oh the *blessedness*, Oh the *happiness*, Oh the *joy* of the poor in spirit, those who mourn, the meek, those who hunger and thirst for righteousness, the merciful, the pure in heart, the peacemakers and those who are persecuted because of righteousness (Matthew 5:3-10). "Rejoice and be glad, because great is your reward in heaven. . ." (Matthew 5:12) ". . . and you will rejoice, and no one will take away your joy" (John 16:22).

Jesus often walked from Nazareth through the Valley of the Doves (upper right) to the town of Magdala (center) on the Sea of Galilee's western shore. From Magdala, he followed the shoreline a few miles north to Capernaum. On the horizon (upper right), the Horns of Hittin overlook the valley. On July 4, 1187, this saddle shaped hill witnessed the massacre of the combined armies of the Crusader Kingdom of Jerusalem at the hands of the conquering Saladin.

Land of the Gergesenes

The northeastern shore of the Sea of Galilee protrudes to form a small peninsula a few miles north of Kibbutz Ein Gev. Although small in area, the land projection can be seen from across the lake. The peninsula forms the mouth of the Wadi Samak, also known as the Valley of Kursi. Measuring only a half mile in width and two miles in length, the valley extends into the lake where it is known locally as "the bank of Kursi." Fishermen know it as the best sardine fishing on the Sea of Galilee.

The valley and underwater bank are the geological result of several merging streams descending from the Golan Heights. The Arabic name of Wadi Samak means "Stream of Fish." The name is no doubt ancient, since the word *samak* also means "fish" in Aramaic (the vernacular of Jesus' time). The modern Hebrew name is Nahal ("stream") Samekh. In ancient Hebrew, the letter "S" (*samekh*) stood for fish.

In Jesus' day, the area of Kursi was under the domain of the Greek city of Hippus, about four miles south of the Wadi Samak. From both an historical perspective and that of the Gospel accounts, it is assumed that a large number of Gentiles lived and worked in this area. Kursi was then known by various names, among them, the Land of *Gadarenes* (Matthew 8:28, NIV/RSV; Mark 5:1, KJV; Luke 8:26, KJV), the Land of *Gergesenes* (Matthew 8:28, KJV), and Land of *Gerasenes* (Mark 5:1, NIV/RSV; Luke 8:26, NIV/RSV). The Gospel writers either did not know or, more likely, did not agree on the precise name of the city.

Use of these variants is confusing since the three names point to three different and widely-separated geographical areas. Not only do differences occur among the Gospel writers, but also within the various manuscripts of each Gospel. These variations, however, caused the early Church fathers little concern. In the late third century (as known from literary sources), they established the site of the

In the late third century, the early Christian fathers established the site of the "swine miracle" at the mouth of Wadi Samak. The wadi (dry rivulet bed) which opens from the valley of Kursi on the northeastern shore of the Sea of Galilee is seen in the background. To commemorate the site, a monastery with a basilica (center foreground) and a small chapel (from which this photo was taken) were built in the early sixth century. After a devastating earthquake in 747 A.D. and complete abandonment of the site at the end of the eighth century, alluvial soil covered the site until its rediscovery in 1969.

The Stones Cry Out

miracle of the swine on the Sea of Galilee's northwestern shore, at the mouth of the Wadi Samak.

Three Jewish sources assist us in choosing the most accurate name. First, the Jerusalem Talmud (interpretation of the Torah — "Law") associates the area around Susita-Hippus with the *Girgashites*, one of the seven Canaanite nations at the time of the Israelite conquest. A similar sounding name, the *Geshurites*, was an Aramaic kingdom on

The ruins of a two-level structure, with walls more than three feet thick, stand halfway up the hill overlooking the ancient basilica. On the upper level, the remnants of a small chapel (see photograph on page 46), with mosaic paving, complete the memorial. The sole surviving white column (center) in the chapel bears a cross in relief, typical of the Byzantine period (325-614 A.D.).

the eastern side of the lake in David's time (1 Samuel 27:8). Finally, the Midrash (commentaries on the Mishna — codified Oral Law), refers to "Gergeshta on the eastern shore of the Sea of Tiberias." Therefore, of the three names mentioned in New Testament manuscripts, the most accurate seems to be *Gergesa*, making the Valley of Kursi, in fact, "the land of the *Gergesenes*."

As with Magdala, Capernaum and Bethsaida, Gergesa gains its prominence from Jesus' activities as described in the Gospels. According to Christian tradition, Gergesa (Kursi) is the site of the healing of the demon-possessed man (or men, according to Matthew). This event, sometimes referred to as the "miracle of the swine" is recorded in the three synoptic Gospels (Matthew 8:28-34, Mark 5:1-20, Luke 8:26-39). The locale is identified with Gergesa (or Gerasa or Gadara), ". . . the region of the Gerasenes, which is across the lake from Galilee" (Luke 8:26).

Following the establishment of Christianity as the official religion of the Roman Empire in the fourth century, churches were built throughout the Holy Land to commemorate Jesus' activities and teaching. It was natural to construct a church to remember the miracle that took place in Kursi. (The church's location remained a mystery until 1969.) The fifth century monk, St. Sabas, described his journey from Beth Shean up the eastern coast of the Sea of Galilee to a place called Chorsia. Upon reaching the site, St. Sabas and his companion prayed in what must have been a church built to commemorate the miracle of the swine. From there they traveled by boat across the lake to Heptapegon, known today as Tabgha.

After the Six Day War in 1969, a team of archaeologists surveyed the Golan region, carefully checking the abandoned Syrian defense village at Kursi. They found no trace of the ancient church. When construction for a new road began in late 1969, surprised workers

Gergesa (Gerasa), a fishing village, lay on the eastern shore between the two hills cutting into the Golan Heights (center). The steep slope to the right of Gergesa is likely where the swine were herded headlong into the sea by demons Jesus cast out of the madman called Legion.

The restored basilica, the centerpiece of the once sizable monastery compound, stands at the foot of the hill associated with Jesus' healing of the demoniac. The well-built structure covers approximately 12,000 square feet. The basilica ends in an apse on its eastern side (left center). A side room on the left side of the photograph contains a restored oil-press that the excavators found in situ (natural or original position). The production of olive oil no doubt provided income for the monastery.

discovered the extensive ruins of this fifth century monastery and church, covering an area of four acres. Thanks to the swift intervention of the noted archaeologist Mendel Nun, the structure remained intact.

Today the excavated church and monastery serve as graphic reminders of the miracle that took place there. Having calmed a turbulent storm while crossing the Sea of Galilee with his disciples (Matthew 8:23-27, Mark 4:35-41, Luke 8:22-25), Jesus arrived on the eastern shore in the Gentile-dominated land of the Gergesenes.

Nearby is the only place where the steep, cavernous hills of the Golan Heights come close to the water. As soon as they stepped ashore, Jesus met a man (or two men according to Matthew) seized with an unclean spirit (Mark) or demons (Luke). Taking the three records into account, there are no doubt two men. Mark and Luke concentrate on what may have been the more vocal or perhaps more violent of the two.

According to Luke, the demoniac wore no clothes and lived among the many limestone caves (some used as tombs) that dot the area. The demons within gave him power to break any chains that were intended to subdue him. Mark notes that night and day he cried out on the mountains and bruised himself with stones. In both Mark and Luke's account, the man identifies himself as Legion "for we are many" (Mark 5:9). (A Roman legion was a regiment of 6,000 troops.)

When he saw Jesus, the demoniac begged him not to torment him. With divine courage and compassion, Jesus commanded the unclean spirits to come out of him. The demons inside the man begged to be allowed to enter a nearby herd of swine, numbering about 2,000 (Mark 5:12-13). Jesus agreed, and the demons left the man and entered the swine, which then "rushed down the steep bank into the lake and were drowned" (Mark 5:13).

The cured demoniac begged to follow Jesus, but Jesus instructed him to go back home "'. . . and tell how much God has done for you.' So the man went away and told all over town how much Jesus had done for him" (Luke 8:39). The madman-turned-missionary proclaimed it even in the cities of the Decapolis — "and all the people were amazed" (Mark 5:20).

The tragedy of the story lies in the conclusion. Those who herded the pigs returned to the town and told what had happened. As a result, the people of Gergesa implored Jesus to leave their territory at once. How like many today whose selfishness callously prevents them from experiencing the wonderful miracles available to the believer.

The truth is, miracles are happening daily. As with Legion, the key to experiencing a miracle is unconditional surrender to Christ. John Gowans' song reminds us of this glorious, simple truth:

> All that you need is a miracle,
> And all that you need can be yours;
> All that you need is available,
> The moment you turn to the Lord.

"When the demons came out of the man, they went into the pigs, and the herd rushed down the steep bank into the lake and was drowned" (Luke 8:33).

The Stones Cry Out

Caesarea Philippi

How good and pleasant it is when brothers

live together in unity! . . . It is as if the dew of

Hermon were falling on Mount Zion. . . .

— Psalm 133:1,3

The Stones Cry Out

S ince biblical times Mount Hermon has marked the northern boundary of Palestine. Its majestic, towering, snow-capped peaks provided protection and life-sustaining water to ancient Israel, and continue to do so today.

Hermon, a Hebrew word meaning "sacred mountain," aptly defines its vital function. Without Mount Hermon, most of Israel would be an uninhabitable, barren desert. Cascading from the summit, melting snow forms three foothill streams. These sparkling tributaries merge a few miles from Banias to become the Jordan River. The Psalmist appropriately sings of Hermon's prominence and benefit (Psalm 89:12, 133:3).

The town of Banias lies in the beautiful hill country on the southern slopes of Mount Hermon about 25 miles north of the Sea of Galilee. Strategically located on the road leading from Kiryat Shmona to the Golan Heights, the ancient hamlet lies near the spring of the Hermon River. This river is one of the three sources of the Jordan River. *Banias* is the Arabic mispronunciation of *Paneas*, the city's ancient name. Since the letter "P" is absent from the Arabic alphabet, *Paneas* has become *Banias*.

Near the spot where the spring gushes out of the reddish-grey stone cliffs, the remains of a shrine to the pastoral deity Pan are visible. Pan was the Greek god of springs and shepherds. This ancient cult replaced Baal, the Semitic deity mentioned throughout the Old Testament. The cult of Pan flourished on the rock escarpment above Paneas. Several caves and niches mark the area, including the one from which the spring feeding the Hermon River issues.

The Roman Emperor Augustus presented the city of Paneas to

Opposite page: The spring of Banias, located at the foot of Mount Hermon in the area of ancient Caesarea Philippi, is the source of the Hermon River, one of three rivers that join to form the Jordan River.

In Jesus' time, the Spring of Banias gushed from this vast ancient cave. The Romans glibly referred to the immense cavern as "the Gates of Hell."

King Herod the Great. In honor of the emperor, Herod built an elaborate palace, of which only fragments remain today. After King Herod's death in 4 B.C., his son Philip became ruler of the region and made Paneas his capital. Philip further beautified the city and renamed it **Caesarea Philippi** to distinguish it from the other Caesarea on the Mediterranean coast. Caesarea Philippi is the city mentioned in Matthew 16:13-20 and Mark 8:27-30 and is the northern most point visited by Jesus and his disciples.

In the fourth century A.D. Caesarea Philippi became a bishopric. It remained a prominent Christian center until the city fell to the conquering Arabs in the seventh century. Its importance increased in the Crusader (1099-1165) and Mameluke (1250-1517) periods, when it was surrounded by a sturdy wall and towers. From the time the Mamelukes captured the town in 1165 it remained an Arab village until 1967.

Jesus may have journeyed to Caesarea Philippi due to the very fact that the population was largely Gentile. In this non-threatening, pastoral setting Jesus would have the peace and quiet needed to prepare his disciples for his rapidly approaching suffering, death and resurrection.

Not far from the pagan votive niches and the immense cave that the Romans referred to as "the Gates of Hell" (see Matthew 16:18), the Lord confronted his disciples with a perplexing concern. Does anyone truly understand him? When asked the direct question, "Who do you say I am?" Simon Bar-Jonah promptly replied, "You are the Christ, the Son of the living God" (Matthew 16:15-16). This divinely-given insight was higher than the contemporary Pharisaic view that regarded the Messiah only as a man exalted to the messianic office (Matthew 22:41-46). Jesus immediately commended Simon's confession. Using a play on words, Jesus declared, ". . . thou art Peter (*petros*), and upon this rock (*petra*) I will build my church; and the gates of hell shall not prevail against it" (Matthew 16:18, KJV).

By his confession Peter identified himself with Christ, the true Rock (1 Corinthians 3:11, 1 Peter 2:4-5). Peter thus became a rock (*petros*). On "*this* rock" (*petra*), however, Jesus proclaimed he would

An elaborate votive niche, surmounted by a decorative conch, may have contained the statue of the god Pan. Under it is a Greek inscription mentioning the nymph Echo and Diopan, the Greek god, "lover of music."

build his glorious and victorious church. Peter and the other apostles, joined by faith in "the chief cornerstone" (Ephesians 2:20), compose "this rock" (*petra*).

From Caesarea Philippi Jesus ascended "a high mountain" and "there he was transfigured before them" (Matthew 17:1-2). Tradition places the transfiguration at Mount Tabor in the Jezreel Valley. It is more likely that the transfiguration took place just above Caesarea Philippi on a spur of Mount Hermon.

These extraordinary events present a dramatic picture. The transient, penniless Galilean carpenter from Nazareth is surrounded by twelve very ordinary followers, and together they discuss and experience the glory and mystery of the Father and his incarnate Son. It is as if Jesus deliberately set himself and his disciples against the backdrop of the world's religions and nature's splendor to illustrate and authenticate his divine identity.

O that Christ's contemporary disciples will continue building the kingdom stone by stone, life by life, with the timeless assurance that "the gates of Hades will not overcome it" (Matthew 16:18). We build on a firm foundation! — "For no one can lay any foundation other than the one already laid, which is Jesus Christ" (1 Corinthians 3:11).

Vacationing Israelis and tourists from around the world savor pleasant moments of spiritual and physical refreshment at the Jordan River's source in Banias.

The Stones Cry Out

Bethany

The Stones Cry Out

One of several small villages known collectively as the "daughters of Judah" (Psalm 48:11, KJV/RSV), Bethany lies on the lower eastern slope of the Mount of Olives. Though modest in size, the village strategically lies on the much-traveled Jerusalem-Jericho road "less than two miles from Jerusalem" (John 11:18).

Initially occupied in the sixth century B.C. (Persian Period), Bethany is first mentioned by the prophet Nehemiah (11:32). The seer mentions three villages around Jerusalem — Anathoth, three miles north of Jerusalem; Nob, on Mount Scopus and Ananiah, also known as Bethananiah. Continuously settled since Nehemiah's time, Bethany is still the last stop on the Jericho road before entering Jerusalem.

Bethany today remains a dilapidated village called el-Azareyeh, an Arabic version of the name Lazarus, its most famous inhabitant. Surrounded with fig, almond and olive trees, clusters of humble Arab dwellings house typically large and often poor families.

The name Bethany originates from the Hebrew *Beth'a-ni*, meaning "House of the Poor" or "House of the Afflicted." The affluent of Jesus' day preferred the protection and services found only in the city. Unlike today, the first century aristocracy migrated *from* the villages *to* the cities. To be sure, Jerusalem had its share of poor. The surrounding villages, however, provided a haven for the destitute. As far back as Nehemiah's time, Bethany claimed recognition as one of Jerusalem's poorest suburbs.

Lazarus, Mary and Martha were the exception to the rule as they resisted the temptation to move to the city. They were likely the only prosperous family living among Bethany's poor. The fact that Mary freely emptied expensive perfume on Jesus' feet (John 12:3) attests to their wealth. In addition, they owned a personal tomb. Family tombs were popular with the wealthy since the poor buried their loved ones in reusable tombs. After twelve months and a day the bones were removed to provide room for another body. This is perhaps one reason Jesus loved the three so much. Their wealth did not deter them from living among the poor. After all, it is likely one of their friends was a *leper* named Simon (Matthew 26:6-13; compare with Mark 14:1-11 and John 12:1-8)!

Bethany justifiably may be called the Judean home of Jesus. He preferred lodging in Bethany to Jerusalem. As friends and admirers of Jesus, Lazarus and his two sisters often welcomed him into their home. On one occasion, however, Jesus' presence caused friction between the sisters. Martha busily served the Lord a meal while Mary, neglecting her household chores, reclined at his feet mesmerized by his teaching (Luke 10:38-42).

Undoubtedly, the most remarkable event occurring in Bethany

Under the present street level stands the closed first century entrance to Lazarus' tomb.

was the resurrection of Lazarus from the dead (John 11). Scholars generally consider the Tomb of Lazarus an authentic site. It conforms to the biblical description and is the only house-tomb discovered in this ancient village.

The sepulcher itself was hewn in rock within a natural cave. The Moslems sealed the original ground level entrance and built a mosque between an ancient church and the tomb. In the seventeenth century, the Franciscans obtained permission to make a new entrance which today leads down to the crypt. The Moslems, however, still maintain the Tomb of Lazarus.

The tomb's existing entrance is from the street on the north side of the cave. Inside the doorway twenty-two steps lead down into the vestibule of the tomb. From here two steps descend into a narrow passage leading into the inner chamber (7½ by 8 feet) of the tomb itself. Lazarus' family placed him in this inner tomb. As John precisely describes, ". . . It was a cave and a stone lay *upon* it" (John 11:38, KJV). A large, flat rectangular stone placed horizontally over the entrance concealed the steps leading to the sepulcher beneath the cavern's floor.

The wrapped and limp body of Lazarus laid on the cold damp floor for four days. Jesus arrived from across the Jordan River where he had

Road leading from Bethany over the Mount of Olives. There is little doubt that this is the road Jesus traveled from Bethany to Jerusalem on Palm Sunday.

The Stones Cry Out

revisited the place where John baptized him (John 10:40-42). Both Mary and Martha met Jesus outside the village and lamented that he had not arrived in time to save their brother's life.

After comforting the sisters, Jesus came to the tomb and ordered the stone covering removed. He stood above the entrance, and through a small opening in the side of the inner tomb he called in a loud voice, "Lazarus, come out!" (John 11:43). Those nearby were astonished to see Lazarus, still wearing his grave shroud, ascend the few steps from the inner tomb. Jesus' words to Martha now brimmed with the lifegiving truth — ". . . I am the resurrection and the life. He who believes in me will live, even though he dies; and whoever lives and believes in me will never die. . . ." (John 11:25-26).

Six days before the Feast of Passover, Jesus made his final visit to Bethany as guest in the house of Simon the leper (Mark 14:3). Mary, Martha and the resurrected Lazarus were present. In a lavish gesture of love, the devoted Mary anointed Jesus with precious ointment, wiping his feet with her hair. Judas Iscariot, along with other un-named disciples, complained that the wasted balm could have been sold and given to the poor who lived all around them(compare Mark 14:1-11 with John 12:1-8). Jesus defended Mary's act as a sign of his

Above left: The natural cave floor opening to the lower sepulcher over which the stone covering Jesus ordered removed was placed.

Above right: The author depicts how Jesus would have called forth Lazarus through an opening in the side of the inner tomb while standing next to the tomb's floor level opening.

coming death (Mark 14:3-9).

From Bethany Jesus walked with his disciples the two miles over the Mount of Olives to Jerusalem where the final episodes leading to his crucifixion and resurrection took place.

Following several appearances and discourses with his disciples, the resurrected Lord returned to the Mount of Olives for his earthly departure. The Ascension took place on the Mount of Olives "out to the vicinity of Bethany" (Luke 24:50-51).

Surely, he will walk Bethany's ancient narrow paths again when he returns. ". . . Even so, come, Lord Jesus" (Revelation 22:20, KJV).

The street level entrance to Lazarus' Tomb in Bethany.

The Stones Cry Out

Jerusalem

Ten measures of beauty descended to the world.
Nine were taken by Jerusalem - and one by the rest
of the world.

— Talmud: *Kiddushim* 49b

The Stones Cry Out

JERUSALEM, the Eternal City, revered by the three great monotheistic religions—Judaism, Christianity and Islam—is the holiest place on earth. A bustling modern metropolis of over a half-million inhabitants, Jerusalem adeptly preserves its special atmosphere of a holy city. The city abounds with places of worship that incorporate memories of the global, life-changing events which have occurred in this unique place.

Ascending to Jerusalem, the contemporary pilgrim follows a well-worn path. Here walked the forebears of the Jewish people — Sarah and Abraham, Rebecca and Isaac, Leah, Rachel and Jacob. Kings David, Solomon and Hezekiah traversed these same roads, as did the conquering Assyrians, Babylonians, Persians, Greeks and Romans.

Jerusalem is not only an ancient city, it is one of the few cities continuously inhabited for more than 4,000 years! Over these four millennia, the city has been destroyed and rebuilt over seventy times. Yet, for each traveler, the timeless beauty of Jerusalem rejuvenates itself.

The beginnings of Jerusalem go back to 3500 - 3000 B.C. when people first settled near the Gihon Spring (Spring of the Virgin) that

Opposite page: A panoramic view of the "Eternal City" from the Mount of Olives.

The octagonal Dome of the Rock dominates the elevated platform in the center of the esplanade of the Temple Mount. Since the seventh century A.D., the golden-domed Islamic shrine has been Jerusalem's most famous landmark. The Western Wall ("Wailing Wall") is a small section of the buttress-wall that surrounded the Temple complex built by King Herod in the first century B.C. It is the holy place most venerated by Jews, since it is the only remnant of the Second Temple that was destroyed by the Romans in 70 A.D.

Jerusalem

An Hassidic ("pious, righteous") Jew prays at the Western Wall. Throughout the ages, Jews have come here to pray and express their grief over the destruction of the Temple and their hope for the Temple's restoration upon the Messiah's coming. Because the Western Wall was the scene of so much lamentation and weeping it became known by non-Jews as the "Wailing Wall."

flows from the Kidron Valley. Egyptian records of the nineteenth century B.C. first mention Jerusalem by the name *Rushalimum*. During this period, Melchizedek, king of Salem and "priest of the most high God," met Abraham (Genesis 14:18-20). From early times Jerusalem was a place of sanctity.

Although the tribe of Judah succeeded in taking Jerusalem from the Canaanites (Judges 1:8), they could not hold on to it. Soon after its capture, the Jebusites seized Jerusalem. They were a strong people, and the tribe of Benjamin "did not drive out the Jebusites that inhabited Jerusalem" (Judges 1:21). The Jebusites remained in Jerusalem until David conquered the city around 1000 B.C. (2 Samuel 5:6-10, 1 Chronicles 11:4-9).

King Solomon constructed the First Temple as directed by God on Mount Moriah, "where the Lord had appeared to his father David. It was on the threshing floor of Araunah the Jebusite, the place provided by David" (2 Chronicles 3:1). Nebuchadnezzar destroyed Solomon's Temple in 586 B.C. Zerubbabel and the returning exiles built a modest Second Temple in 515 B.C.

Herod the Great (37-4 B.C.) enlarged and beautified the Second Temple. It became one of the wonders of the ancient world. The Roman General, Titus, demolished Herod's Temple in 70 A.D., leaving intact only the Western Wall, Jewry's holiest shrine.

It was Herod's greatly expanded and splendidly restored Temple that Jesus knew and loved. After all, Jerusalem was his Father's chosen city and the Temple his earthly residence. Here Jehovah *dwelt* with his people.

As an observant Jew, Jesus made his way to Jerusalem and the

The Blessing of the Priests is annually observed at the Western Wall during Passover.

The Stones Cry Out

The western wall is considered a synagogue and is therefore a place for studying the Torah and theological discussion.

Temple a minimum of three times a year for the "pilgrimage festivals" (Luke 2:42). Mosaic Law required that all physically able and cere–monially clean male Jews attend the Feast of Unleavened Bread (Passover), the Feast of Pentecost and the Feast of Tabernacles annu-ally (Deuteronomy 16:16). Since Jesus came to fulfill the Law, he faithfully attended the required and, at times, the optional feasts (John 10:22).

A thirteen year old boy comes to manhood as a result of his Bar Mitzvah *("Son of the Commandment"). Jewish families from around the world travel to the Western Wall for this sacred ceremony.*

Since the Temple area has been reconstructed only four times in history, today's traveler can actually walk on steps that once sup-ported our Lord's sandal-clad feet. The pilgrim can touch immense limestone ashlars (building stones) which heard the whimpers of six-week old *Y'shua* ("Jesus") as Mary nervously presented him to Simeon and Anna. Three decades later, these stones witnessed Jesus' often fervid dialogue with the religious leaders of his day. They once reverberated with the Lord's penetrating condemnation of those who had turned his Father's House into "a den of robbers" (Matthew 21:13).

Jerusalem provided the backdrop for Jesus' miracles and clashes with the Pharisees, the triumphal entry on Palm Sunday and the final meal with his disciples in the Upper Room. Following his mock trial and condemnation, Jesus dragged the cross through the narrow, uneven *Via Dolorosa* to the site of his crucifixion, burial and resurrec-

Another Jewish day begins as night descends on the Eternal City.

tion. Through times of glorious triumph and in the face of apparent tragedy, Jesus never lost compassion for the Eternal City or its inhabitants. His constant hope and prayer was for their salvation. "'O Jerusalem, Jerusalem,' he lamented, 'you who kill the prophets and stone those sent to you, how often I have longed to gather your children together, as a hen gathers her chicks under her wings, but you were not willing'" (Matthew 23:37).

As Jesus' contemporary disciples, we too must love and pray for "the city of our God" (Psalm 48:1,8). Now, perhaps more than ever before, the psalmist's entreaty rings with urgency — *Sha'a'lu' shalom Yerushalayim* — "Pray for the peace of Jerusalem. . ." (Psalm 122:6).

This is what the Lord says: "I will return to Zion and dwell in Jerusalem. Then Jerusalem will be called the City of Truth, and the mountain of the Lord Almighty will be called the Holy Mountain . . . Once again men and women of ripe old age will sit in the streets of Jerusalem, each with cane in hand because of his age. The city streets will be filled with boys and girls playing there." — Zechariah 8:35

The Stones Cry Out

The Temple Mount

The land of Israel is at the center of the world; Jerusalem is at the center of the land of Israel; the Temple is at the center of Jerusalem...

—Midrash Tanhuma: *Kedoshim* 10

The Stones Cry Out

The Temple Mount is sacred to Christians, Jews and Moslems. The world's three great religions identify it as Mount Moriah, the place where Abraham attempted to offer his son as a sacrifice to God (Genesis 22).

For the Jews, the Temple Mount is also the site of the two splendid Temples of Israel. So exquisite were these structures that the Jewish sages declared, "He who has not seen the Temple of Israel has never in his life seen a beautiful structure" (Talmud: *Baba Bathra* 4). Today, a sign near the Dung Gate warns the orthodox not to enter the Temple area to avoid accidentally walking on the *Debir* ("Holy of Holies"), forbidden to all but the high priest on the Day of Atonement (Leviticus 16).

Christians revere the Temple Mount as the place Jesus frequently visited; where he often confronted his adversaries and taught his disciples (see Mark 11-13).

The history of the Temple Mount goes back nearly four millennia to the time of Abraham. God tested the Patriarch, instructing him to ". . . Take your son, your only son, Isaac, whom you love, and go to the region of Moriah. Sacrifice him there as a burnt offering on one of the mountains I will tell you about" (Genesis 22:2).

Eight centuries later, God directed King David to build a temple to house the Ark of the Covenant. The Prophet Gad told David to ". . . Go up and build an altar to the Lord on the threshing floor of Araunah the Jebusite. . . So David bought the threshing floor and the oxen and paid fifty shekels of silver for them" (2 Samuel 24:18,24). Most scholars believe that Araunah's threshing floor (large flat tract of bedrock) was

Opposite page: Crowned by the crescent of Islam and framed by one of the graceful archways of its eight approaches, Jerusalem's glistening Dome of the Rock has changed little since its construction 1300 years ago.

The southeastern corner of the Temple Mount as viewed from the Mount of Olives. The Dome of the Rock (right center)) and the El Aqsa Mosque (left) have dominated the Temple Mount since the seventh century A.D. First century steps leading from the Second Temple (Herod's Temple) can be seen just below the El Aqsa Mosque.

The southern wall of the Temple Mount as depicted in the model of first century Jerusalem on the grounds of the Holyland Hotel. The Tyropean Valley winds its way through the center of the picture with the "City of David" to its right.

The Temple of Jesus day (Second Temple) as reconstructed in the model of first century Jerusalem. Michael Avi-Yonah, the renowned biblical topographer, was commissioned to render the model of what Jerusalem must have looked like "at the time of the Second Temple, shortly after the rule of Herod the Great" — in other words, at the time of Jesus.

located on the crest of Mount Moriah.

King David prepared the plans and material for the Temple (1 Chronicles 22:1-19,28:1-21;29:1-9), but it was his brilliant son, King Solomon, whom God allowed to build the First Temple on Mount Moriah. Using brass, copper and cedars from Lebanon (the latter sent by King Hiram of Tyre), Solomon's craftsmen labored seven years to finish the Temple. King Solomon dedicated his magnificent Temple in his eleventh year, ca. 950 B.C. With its completion, the twelve tribes had a political, religious and cultural center in Jerusalem.

In 586 B.C., the Babylonian King Nebuchadnezzar ravaged Jerusalem, destroying Solomon's Temple. Charred stones excavated from the "Burnt Room" on the Hill Ophel near the Temple Mount, remain salient testimony to this devastating conflagration. Fifty years later (536 B.C.), Cyrus, the Persian king, permitted the Jews to return to Jerusalem under the leadership of Zerubbabel. Zerubbabel, the appointed governor, along with Joshua the high priest, led nearly 50,000 Jews back to the Eternal City for the chief purpose of rebuilding the Temple (Ezra 3-6). Upon reaching Jerusalem, they set up the altar of burnt offering and proceeded to lay the foundation for a new Temple. The ever-present adversaries of the Jewish people, however, succeeded in delaying further work on the Temple for sixteen years. In 520 B.C., with the encouragement of prophets Haggai and Zechariah, the work resumed. Zerubbabel completed the Second Temple four years later in 516 B.C. Although a great celebration was held to dedicate the new temple (Ezra 6:16-22), the elderly wept when they remembered the glory of the First Temple (Ezra 3:12).

The Temple Mount today is essentially the same size as that of

Herod the Great's (37-4 B.C.) grandiose expansion of the Second Temple constructed by Zerubbabel. While some logically refer to Herod's Temple as the *Third Temple*, the rabbis have always contended that the despised King Herod only renovated Zerubbabel's Temple.

Commenced in 37 B.C., the colossal, expanded Temple was not dedicated until 10 A.D., fourteen years after Herod's death. A tyrannical master builder, Herod employed 10,000 workmen, thousands of priests and the foremost engineers of the Roman Empire for the task. He doubled the extent of the existing Temple Mount by lengthening the eastern wall at both ends and by building new walls on the remaining three sides. He added a monumental Stoa (Greek portico) over the Court of the Gentiles along the extended southern wall, a bridge connecting the Temple Mount with the Upper City, splendid stairways leading to and from the southern and southwestern walls and the imposing Antonio Fortress to guard the Temple Mount's vulnerable northern wall. Herod's lavish renovation covered an area of about forty acres, one-sixth the size of the entire city.

Barely a generation after the completion of Herod the Great's grand undertaking, the Roman general and future emperor, Titus, suppressed a protracted Jewish rebellion (66-70 A.D.). Under his command, the Roman Tenth Legion utterly destroyed Jerusalem and the Temple Mount. Titus ordered that the mighty retaining walls remain standing as a testimony to Rome's devastation of the Jewish capital. Subsequent empires caused the steady deterioration of the retaining wall by using the Herodian ashlars (building stones) to build new structures. The only surviving remnant of the Temple today is the *Kotel*, Hebrew for the southwestern section of the retaining wall known as the Western Wall.

The famed Western Wall is the most holy site for Jews throughout the world. This venerated wall has been the focus of Jewish prayer for centuries. It is the place where Jews express their grief over the destruction of the Temple, their long exile and their hope for the eventual return of Temple worship. Because the Western Wall was the scene of so much lamentation and weeping, non-Jews referred to it as the "Wailing Wall." Immediately following the destruction of the Second Temple, the sages declared that the *Shechinah* ("The Presence of God") will never leave the Western Wall. According to the rabbis, "God made an oath that this wall will never be destroyed."

A partition perpendicular to the first century wall separates men and women since the Western Wall is considered a synagogue. It is customary for visitors (both Jews and Gentiles) to write their inmost prayer on a piece of paper and insert it between the huge stone ashlars. These written prayers are considered sacred and will never be dis-

Original stones of the monumental Herodian stairway that stretched 215 feet across the southern wall of the Temple Mount. As was the custom, Jesus would stop to converse with his disciples on these "teaching steps." The Scribes and Pharisees often eavesdropped and posed their own questions to Jesus. Without doubt, the Master Teacher walked and taught on these very steps.

The Stones Cry Out

The model of the "Teaching Steps" leading from the double Hulda Gates. The steps were constructed of wide, smooth, closely fitting limestone paving blocks. Set alternately in wide and narrow rows to discourage running, the thirty step stairway ascends 22 feet to the upper street that passed along the length of the southern wall.

carded. Periodically, the rabbis remove the prayers from the crevices and bury them in special boxes on the Mount of Olives.

The Israeli government greatly enlarged and deepened the area in front of the Western Wall following the 1967 Six Day War. The exposed part of the wall today is about 200 feet long. The seven lowest courses of the wall are the original Herodian section. Under the pavement, eight more courses of Herodian stones extend down to a first century paved street that ran along the Western Wall from north to south. Under this subterranean street are nine more layers of foundation stones.

Since the seventh century A.D., the octagonal Dome of the Rock has dominated the elevated platform in the center of the esplanade of the Temple Mount. This sacred shrine of Islam (not a mosque) encloses the rock upon which Abraham was to sacrifice his son. The *Koran* (sacred book of Islam) teaches that Ishmael, not Isaac, was the intended sacrifice. The protruding limestone bedrock is identified on medieval maps *as-Sahra*, the center of the world. Moslems also believe that the rock contains a depression caused by the hoof of al-Burak, the winged horse that flew Mohammed to heaven from this spot.

Soon after regaining control of the Temple Mount on June 7, 1967, the Israeli government began excavations on the southern wall. The acclaimed archaeologist Professor Benjamin Mazar conducted the excavation that lasted ten years. He uncovered substantial remains from five major archaeological periods at the foot of the Temple Mount. The entire excavation is now an archaeological park. Visitors may walk through and around Ommayad, Byzantine, Herodian, Hasmonean and First Temple remains.

The Temple Mount

Professor Mazar's greatest discovery was the expansive Herodian staircase that led to the triple-arched entrance and double-arched exit known as the Hulda Gates. The staircase is 215 feet wide, containing 30 steps that alternate between wide and narrow steps to discourage running. Without question, Jesus ascended these steps each time he entered the Temple, pausing first to purify himself in one of the many *mikva'ot* ("ritual baths") at the base of the staircase. Since it was the custom for rabbis to teach their followers on the steps leading from the double-arched gate, Jesus doubtless paused here often to teach the Twelve. It is fair to assume that Jesus also may have used this ideal location to preach to the multitudes (see Matthew 23 and John 7:37-44).

The numerous ritual immersion baths (*mikva'ot*) near the entrance to the Temple Mount likely witnessed another prominent New Testament event recorded in Acts, chapter two. Following the outpouring of the Holy Spirit on the day of Pentecost, 3,000 people received Peter's message and were baptized that day. The event begs the question, "Where in Jerusalem would there be sufficient water to baptize this large number of converts?" It is probable that Peter preached his well-known Pentecost sermon on the Temple steps. The nearby *mikva'ot*, which served the thousands of pilgrims streaming into Jerusalem for the annual feasts, easily could have met the needs of this relatively small assembly of believers in *Y'shua* ("Jesus").

The excitement of standing on the Temple's broad staircase affords an ineffable personal moment. At that moment, the glorious, transcendent reality emerges ever so clearly. One need not come to Jerusalem to meet the God of the Temple or the Christ of history or the Spirit of Pentecost. He is as close as the whisper of the seeker's prayer.

Remnants of the Herodian steps and the double Hulda Gate exit from the southern wall. Note the small remaining fragment of the Double Gate arch above the stairway in the center left of the picture.

The Stones Cry Out

Pools of Healing

The Old and New Testaments mention the Pool of Bethesda and the Pool of Siloam. These pools were thought to have healing powers. *Berekhah*, the Hebrew word for "pool," is an expansion of its root "to bless." *Berekhah* refers to an artificial pool constructed to conserve water for irrigation and drinking.

Only the Apostle John records the two remarkable miracles associated with these ancient pools (John 5:1-15, 9:1-41). While not discrediting the popular superstitions associated with these reservoirs, Jesus seized the opportunity to perform two of his well-known miracles.

The Pool of Bethesda lies a few hundred yards from St. Stephen's Gate (also known as the Lion's Gate). This ancient entrance penetrates the eastern wall of the Old City of Jerusalem just above the northeast corner of the Temple Mount. At the time of Christ, this area was just outside the northern wall of the city near the Sheep Gate leading into the Temple.

While various New Testament manuscripts give three names to the pool, *Bethesda*, meaning "House of Mercy," is most commonly used. Once fed by rain water and ancient aqueducts, the Pool of Bethesda is now dried up. In Jesus' time the pool was a meeting place for invalids who believed that the water possessed healing properties. They faithfully awaited the release of its healing power "when the water (was) stirred" (John 5:7).

Buried under debris for centuries, the impressive remnants of the pool were unearthed by French archaeologists during extensive excavations begun in 1956. They discovered that the pool was rectangular in shape (about 350 feet long by 200 feet wide by 25 feet deep), surrounded on all four sides by porches. A fifth portico divided the

Excavations just northeast of the Church of St. Anne uncovered remnants of the Pool of Bethesda. Here Jesus healed a man who had been crippled for 38 years (John 5:1-15).

The Stones Cry Out

The Pool of Bethesda in Jesus' day as reconstructed in the model of first century Jerusalem located on the grounds of the Holyland Hotel. Note the five porches (four sides plus the middle porch) as described in John 5:2.

pool in the middle. These findings confirmed John's description of the pool as having five porticos.

John is always careful to point out that Jesus observed the obligations of Jewish worship. On this occasion, he was again in Jerusalem for an unnamed feast.

Jesus' disciples are absent from the narrative. Thus, it may be that he was alone as he walked among the disabled. Perhaps someone pointed out the man who had been crippled for 38 years. The invalid's decrepit condition made it unlikely, if not impossible, for him to be the first to reach the pool's moving water. He needed someone to help him. Jesus recognized his implicit faith and intense desire for healing. He commanded him to ". . . 'Get up! Pick up your mat and walk.' At once the man was cured; he picked up his mat and walked" (John 5:8-9).

Because Jesus performed this miracle on the Sabbath, it is not surprising that the divine act inflamed the Jewish leaders. "For this reason the Jews tried all the harder to kill him; not only was he breaking the Sabbath, but he was even calling God his own Father, making himself equal with God" (John 5:18).

The Pool of Siloam, located on the southwestern corner of the Hill Ophel, also served as a water reservoir. It lay directly below the grand southern entrance to the Temple. The water of the spring of *Gihon* ("gusher"), diverted through Hezekiah's Tunnel (2 Kings 20:20), continually filled the man-made pool. The religious leaders consid-

A mosque's minaret stands sentinel over the remnants of the Pool of Siloam.

A replica of the Pool of Siloam on the grounds of the Holyland Hotel.

ered this crystalline spring water the most pure in Jerusalem and used it in Temple ceremonies. The Feast of Tabernacles began with a solemn procession of priests carrying water from the Pool of Siloam to the Temple.

The formation of this artificial reservoir is the result of one of the monumental engineering feats of ancient history. In the year 701 B.C., King Hezekiah cut a tunnel through the limestone rock of the hill Ophel ("City of David") to convey water from the Gihon Spring. The spring, located outside the city walls, then would empty its waters into the Pool of Siloam, within the walls of the city. Although some archaeologists suspect that Hezekiah's engineers followed fractures in the rock, no one knows for certain how this herculean task was accomplished.

King Hezekiah undertook this unparalleled project to protect the city's precious water supply from the invading Assyrian army. Hezekiah then closed and hid the outlet from Sennacherib, king of Assyria (2 Chronicles 32:1-4). Discouraged by thirst and pestilence, the Assyrians eventually withdrew and failed to conquer the Eternal City.

In the days of Jesus, people mistakenly considered the Pool of Siloam a self-generating spring. The well-known historian, Josephus Flavius, attests this fact. The passage of time had caused this misconception. Although the water of the Gihon Spring continued to seep into the pool, by the first century Hezekiah's Tunnel was concealed and long forgotten. The Pool of Siloam was regarded a spring until the American orientalist Edward Robinson discovered and traversed Hezekiah's Tunnel in 1837 — an adventure anyone can experience today.

John alone records the healing of the blind man using the agency of the Pool of Siloam (John 9). Since the setting for John 7-9 is the great Feast of Tabernacles, Jesus may have met the blind man on the steps leading from the Temple's southern exit. The steps made an ideal tiered classroom, and it was not unusual for a rabbi to pause on these "teaching steps" to instruct his disciples.

On this occasion, the disciples asked Jesus a perplexing theological question. Since they knew that this man had been blind from birth, they asked, "Rabbi, who sinned, this man or his parents, that he was born blind?" (John 9:2). Since rabbinic teaching connected suffering and sin, how could blindness possibly be due to his own sin, when he had been blind from his birth? Jesus explained that physical infirmity has no direct connection to sin, but can instead be a means to manifest the glory of God (John 9:3-5).

Jesus then made clay with his own spittle and spread it on the

Opposite page: Completing a refreshing half hour walk through Hezekiah's Tunnel, a group emerges in what remains of the Pool of Siloam.

The Stones Cry Out

Pools of Healing

Recently discovered remnants of the Tower of Siloam. Named after the nearby Pool of Siloam, this tower was part of Jerusalem's ancient fortifications. The collapse of the tower resulted in the death of eighteen persons. Jesus used this tragedy as an object lesson during his teaching on repentance: ". . . those eighteen who died when the tower in Siloam fell on them - do you think they were more guilty than all the others living in Jerusalem?" (Luke 13:4).

man's eyes. Perhaps pointing south, he ordered the man to, "'Go, wash in the Pool of Siloam'. . . So the man went and washed, and came home seeing" (John 9:7).

As with the healing of the crippled man by the Pool of Bethesda, Jesus performed this miracle on the Sabbath (John 9:16), causing another confrontation with the Pharisees. Indeed, Jesus endured perpetual conflict with the religious leaders, the middle class, of first-century Jewish society.

In both encounters by these famous pools, Christ asked the one in need of healing to do the impossible. On the surface the requests were outlandish. To the man lame for 38 years Jesus commanded, "Pick up your bed and walk" — *preposterous!* To the man blind from birth Christ instructed him to find his way to the Pool of Siloam before he would see — *absurd!* **FAITH** alone makes the difference. The old gospel chorus reminds us of this eternal truth:

> *Faith, mighty faith, the promise sees and looks to that alone; laughs at impossibilities and cries: "It shall be done!"*

The Stones Cry Out

The Upper Room

The pyramidal grey-domed Dormition Abbey (far left on the horizon) sets on what today is known as Mount Zion. The Upper Room and Tomb of David are adjacent to the abbey.

The Madaba mosaic, the earliest known map of the Holy Land, is located in a church in Madaba, Jordan. The famed map depicts Jerusalem as it appeared in the sixth century. The Roman Emperor Hadrian constructed the long colonnaded central street known as the "cardo" (heart). At the far right of this street stand two red-roofed buildings. The larger structure, on the left, with yellow doors and triangular gable, is the Hagia Sion basilica. Adjacent to its right, the smaller structure with a white door is the Church of the Apostles that was built over the Judeo-Christian synagogue on Mount Zion. This church/synagogue marks the site of the Last Supper and Pentecost. Remnants of this first century structure are incorporated into the present wall of the so-called Tomb of David.

On the southwestern hill of Jerusalem, today called Mount Zion, next to the imposing grey-domed Dormition Abbey, stand the remains of the earliest Judeo-Christian synagogue, later known as the Church of the Apostles. Naturally, the place where first-century Jewish Christians worshipped was called a synagogue. Jewish believers built this synagogue to mark the place where the apostles prayed following their return from the Mount of Olives after witnessing Christ's ascent to heaven.

Paradoxically, all that remains of the Church of the Apostles is a small chamber traditionally venerated as the tomb of King David. In the 12th century, the Crusaders incorporated the first century walls of this room into the Church of St. Mary. In the room adjoining the so-called Tomb of David, the Crusaders commemorated the place where Jesus washed his disciples' feet (John 13:1-17). Above this room, they built the Chamber of Mysteries, today known by its Latin name *Cenacle* or *Coenaculum* ("dining room"). This chamber marks the Upper Room where Jesus and his disciples celebrated the Passover Meal (Matthew 26:17-30, Mark 14:12-26, Luke 22:7-38) and where the apostles returned following Christ's crucifixion (John 20:19-29) and ascension (Acts 1:12-14). Some days later, the Holy Spirit descended on the disciples assembled in the Upper Room on the day of Pentecost (Acts 2:1-13).

In addition to building a place of worship, there is evidence that the early Jewish-Christian community established their headquarters on this spot. They associated this church with Isaiah's prophecy — "The law will go out from Zion, the word of the Lord from Jerusalem" (Isaiah 2:3). Thankfully, the church escaped destruction during the

Jewish revolts of 66-70 A.D. and 132-135 A.D. against Rome. This is doubtless because the structure stood outside the area of fighting.

It is ironic that the notoriously anti-Semitic Crusaders mistakenly identified the first-century structure as the tomb of King David. In 1176, they placed the existing stone cenotaph (empty coffin or memorial) in the room. Since then, it has been venerated at various times by Jews, Moslems and Christians. While none of these faiths now consider the Tomb of David authentic, it remains the second most sacred site to the Jews, next to the Western Wall.

The traditional Tomb of David rests on Mount Zion because the scripture indicates that King David was buried *within* the city. According to 1 Kings 2:10, ". . . David rested with his fathers and was buried *in* the City of David." By Jewish law, burials always occurred *outside* the city walls. The only exception to this ordinance in all of Israel's history was the royal line of David to King Ahaz. Since the city which David captured from the Jebusites occupied the Hill Ophel, the southern spur of Mount Moriah, and was then known as Mount Zion, it is certain that King David's resting place remains somewhere on this 11-acre ridge.

The present chamber of the Upper Room is part of the 12th century Crusader church. In the early 16th century, the Moslems turned the Coenaculum into a mosque by adding a *Mihrab* ("prayer niche") in its southern wall. A large Arabic inscription on the wall dating to 1524 commemorates this event and mentions the Ottoman Sultan, Suleiman the Magnificent, who built the present walls of the Old City of Jerusalem. Jews and Christians were prohibited from entering the chamber until 1948.

In the twelfth century, the Crusaders built the Church of St. Mary over the ruins of the Church of the Apostles and the Hagia Sion basilica. Above the walls of the Church of the Apostles, the Crusaders built a second floor, known as the cenacle, to commemorate both the Last Supper and the events during Pentecost described in Acts 2.

The Upper Room

Mount Zion Monastery courtyard. Arriving in the Holy Land between 1335 and 1337, the Franciscan order built a monastery. Parts of the original monastery are still standing, with this courtyard at its center, on Mount Zion. The Moslems forced the Franciscans to abandon the site in the sixteenth century. A Jewish Yeshiva (religious school) now occupies the monastery building.

The Coenaculum, restored in the mid-1980s, preserves many architectural details of the Crusader period. Most notable are the characteristic arched windows. One of the most interesting details is the capital of the column supporting a small canopy covering the stairwell leading to the Tomb of David. Sculptured on the capital are pelicans with folded wings. On each side, a central pelican feeds two young pelicans with its own blood. This portrays the ancient belief that pelicans would, if necessary, feed their offspring with their own blood to the point of sacrificing their life. The legend became a vivid symbol of Christ's sacrificial death.

Although the present structure is only about 900 years old, it is reasonable to assume that the disciples met often on or near this location from the time of the Last Supper through Pentecost. Each of the portentous events recorded by the Gospel writers as taking place in the Upper Room becomes a step in Christ's establishment of his Church.

In the Upper Room, Jesus demonstrated the quintessence of discipleship by washing the apostles' feet prior to celebrating the beginning of Passover. During the Seder (Passover Meal) Jesus tutored them on the significance of his impending death.

In the same room, the resurrected Christ first appeared to his disciples following his encounter with Mary Magdalene earlier in the day. According to the Apostle John, "A week later, his disciples were in the house again. . . Though the doors were locked, Jesus came and stood among them. . ." (John 20:26). Jesus would have used the customary greeting of *Shalom* ("Peace be with you") on both post-resurrection appearances. Without doubt, the well-used salutation gave the disciples special comfort on these occasions.

Following Christ's ascension on the Mount of Olives, the disciples ". . . returned to Jerusalem. . . When they arrived, they went upstairs

The French archaelolgist Raymond Weill, excavating on the eastern hill (Ophel) in 1913, uncovered a number of cave tombs. Weill believed he had uncovered the royal necropolis. Many archaeologists agree that, if this is not exactly where David was buried, it was nearby. His burial must have been in the City of David — on the Hill Ophel (the eastern hill) — overlooking the Kidron Valley.

The Stones Cry Out

A view of the Mount of Offence from within the largest burial cave uncovered by Raymond Weill on the Hill Ophel. This may indeed be a burial chamber for one of the Kings of Judah.

to the room where they were staying" (Acts 1:12-13). After choosing a replacement for the disgraced Judas, the apostles joined with about 120 believers to prepare for the Feast of Pentecost. In the Upper Room on the Day of Pentecost the disciples ". . . were all together in one place. Suddenly a sound like the blowing of a violent wind came from heaven and filled the whole house where they were sitting. They saw what seemed to be tongues of fire that separated and came to rest on each of them. All of them were filled with the Holy Spirit. . ." (Acts 2:1-4).

The sublime events that took place in that first-century Upper Room serve as a perpetual spiritual guide for Christ's disciples throughout the ages. Still today, the Master longs to instruct, encourage and equip his followers in churches around the world. Although the church visible comes in a myriad of shapes, sizes, cultures and languages, the Christ whom they love and serve summons each "flock" to meet him in their "Upper Room."

The Upper Room

Garden of Gethsemane

Rising majestically above the Kidron Valley, the Mount of Olives stands sentinel over Jerusalem. Three hundred feet higher than Jerusalem, its summit offers a spectacular view of the Eternal City to the west; the Judean Hills, the Dead Sea and the majestic mountains of Moab to the east. On this well-known hill Christ foretold the destruction of Jerusalem, taught his disciples how to pray, often came for meditation and prayer and ascended into heaven.

Near the foot of the Mount of Olives, on the western slope above the Kidron Valley, lies the site of the Garden of Gethsemane. This area was heavily wooded in Old Testament times. When Nehemiah restored the Feast of Tabernacles in 445 B.C., he commanded the people to "Go forth unto the mount, and fetch olive branches, and pine branches, and myrtle branches, and palm branches and branches of thick trees, to make booths. . ." (Nehemiah 8:15, KJV).

Well-known in Jesus' day for its spacious natural caves, olive trees and presses, the entire area provided an escape for people seeking relief from the heat of the crowded city streets. Gethsemane (meaning "olive-oil press") was in reality the "city park" of first-century Jerusalem.

For Christian pilgrims, the Garden of Gethsemane is one of the most significant sites in the Holy Land. This garden-park became a habitual rendezvous for the small group of Jesus' disciples who passed it regularly on their way in and out of Jerusalem. As John crisply notes, ". . . Jesus had often met there with his disciples" (John 18:2). With only olive trees and sleepy disciples for companions, our Lord retreated to his favorite spot in the garden to spend the last agonizing hours before his betrayal and predawn arrest.

Little remains of the original garden, and most of the area is now the site of various churches. Next to the Church of All Nations (Church of the Agony), however, is a well-kept garden where eight ancient olive trees survive. Botanists confirm that the roots of these robust trees are well over 1,000 years old. While certitude is impos-

Below left: A view of Jerusalem's eastern wall from the Mount of Olives across the Kidron Valley. Jewish graves stretch "like white-washed tombs" (Matthew 23:27) across the foreground. At the base of the hill (right center) is the area of the Garden of Gethsemane.

Below right: The winding road from the Garden of Gethsemane (upper left) through the Kidron Valley passes the so-called Monument of Absolom (lower center). Following his arrest, Jesus was led along this path to the house of the high priest, Caiaphas.

The Stones Cry Out

sible, some believe that the original shoots of these twisted, gnarled trees witnessed the extraordinary events of that fateful night.

Today, believers the world over come to kneel at the outcrop of rock dominating the altar of the Church of All Nations. A fourth century church originally surrounded this large rock shelf where many believe Jesus prayed in agony to his Father.

The biblical account of Jesus' final week indicates that he was in Bethany at the house of Simon the Leper the night after the triumphal entry. He could have stayed in Bethany for a few nights throughout the week; however, it is also possible that he and the disciples stayed in the Garden of Gethsemane. There were enough natural caves in the garden for him to spend the night if he wished. Shelter was a necessity since March-April is still in the rainy season. John tells us that it was cold on that ominous night (John 18:18).

This was the most sorrowful time of his Passion — the hour in which he trembled in his human form, choosing to suffer and die on

The ornate Monument of Absolom stands at the base of the Kidron Valley directly below the Garden of Gethsemane between the Mount of Olives and the Temple Mount. Because Absolom revolted against his father David, Jewish passersby have thrown stones at the monument site since its erection before the birth of Christ. Parents would bring rebellious children here to impress upon them the consequences of their misconduct.

Garden of Gethsemane

Ancient olive trees, the roots of which are believed to be over 1,000 years old.

the cross, taking upon himself the sins of all mankind. Jesus appealed to his Father, ". . . if thou be willing, remove this cup from me: nevertheless not my will, but thine, be done" (Luke 22:42, KJV). Luke intensifies the pathos of this scene. He describes Jesus sweating as he prays "as it were great drops of blood falling down to the ground" while the disciples were "sleeping for sorrow" (Luke 22: 44-45, KJV).

Seeing beyond the pain, John omits any reference to the agony and sorrow comprising the Son's prayer to his Father. Instead, he underscores Jesus' strength in this time of crisis and decision. In his account of Jesus' arrest, John emphasizes that Jesus seized the initiative by going out to meet his accusers. He totally controlled the subsequent dialogue, at the same time reprimanding his impulsive disciple, Peter (John 18:1-11).

The inevitable moment of his arrest quickly approached. The only chance of arresting Jesus was to choose a time when he would be away from his many supporters; it seemed that "the whole world has gone after him!" (John 12:19).

Without warning, Judas arrived with a large contingent of Temple Guards composed of Levites, officially dispatched by the Sanhedrin. Luke records that some of the chief officers and priests themselves were a part of the clandestine conspiracy (Luke 22:52). According to John 18:3 and 12 the Roman military was also present, underscoring the obvious collusion between Pilate and the Jewish authorities.

Judas led a surprising number of Temple Guards and Roman soldiers to arrest Jesus. The Greek word *speira*, translated *band* (KJV) or *detachment* (NIV) of soldiers, normally referred to a Roman cohort of 600 infantry, one-tenth of a legion. Occasionally, *speira* described a

smaller detachment of 200 men called a *maniple*, or one-thirtieth of a legion. Even if we accept the smaller force, it was a sizable expedition to send against an unarmed Galilean carpenter!

Judas greeted Jesus in a manner still used by students for their rabbi teachers — a kiss. Although not out of the ordinary, this display grieved Jesus (Luke 22:48). He had recognized Satan's voice in Peter's reckless pledge of devotion at Caesarea Philippi only weeks before (Matthew 16:21-23). Jesus now discerned the kiss of betrayal in Judas' impertinent gesture.

It is unlikely the Temple Guard arrested Jesus before 10:30 p.m. It would have been past 11:00 p.m. by the time the company led Jesus across the Kidron and Tyropoeon Valleys to the house of Caiaphas on Mount Zion's eastern slope. Alone in the high priest's basement dungeon, Jesus spent an agonizing sleepless night prior to his formal trial the next morning.

As our Lord resigned himself completely to his Father's will, so

Across the Kidron Valley from the Garden of Gethsemane loom the twin portals of the Golden Gate. Erected in the seventh century A.D. over the Gate Beautiful built by the returnees from Babylon, the Golden Gate was blocked after Saladin conquered Jerusalem in 1187 A.D. The Golden Gate is believed to be the one through which Jesus entered Jerusalem on Palm Sunday.

Garden of Gethsemane

must we. Each petition must conclude with the affirmation "... nevertheless not my will, but thine, be done" (Luke 22:42, KJV). The second stanza of Albert Orsborn's acclaimed hymn "My life must be Christ's broken bread" is a succinct reminder of this Gethsemane principle:

> My all is in the Master's hands
> For him to bless and break;
> Beyond the brook his winepress stands
> And thence my way I take,
> Resolved the whole of love's demands
> To give, for his dear sake.

Sheep graze among ancient olive trees in the area of the Garden of Gethsemane.

The Stones Cry Out

House of Caiaphas

The Church of St. Peter in Gallicantu ("cock-crow") stands on the eastern slope of Mount Zion over the site of what many believe to be the house of the high priest Caiaphas.

Pilgrims to Jerusalem can visit the infamous site where Jesus spent a night of misery in the concealed dungeon of Caiaphas the Jewish high priest. An early visitor, known as the pilgrim of Bourdeaux, authenticates the site. After his visit in 333 A.D. he wrote, "In the same valley of Siloam, you go up to Mount Sion and you see the place where stood the house of Caiaphas. . ."

The probable site of Caiaphas' palatial home sits on Mount Zion's eastern slope above the village of Silwan. The Church of St. Peter in Gallicantu stands over the site. The church's French name literally means "St. Peter-at-the-cock-crow," referring to the apostle Peter's threefold denial of Christ in the palace courtyard.

The church's veranda offers an exceptional view of the lower Kidron Valley. Included in the splendid panorama is the ancient City of David (now the village of Silwan) and the newly-excavated southern entrance to the Temple Mount. Beyond the Temple is the Garden of Gethsemane. The Mount of Olives and Mount of Offence provide a majestic background for this unforgettable scene.

Five steps uncovered in the initial 1888 excavation of the site led to the further discovery of a terraced street leading from the Pool of Siloam. This street existed in Jesus' day. Archaeologists discovered a coin from the Hasmonean period (143-63 B.C.) between cracks in the stairs. Visitors to the church now walk on these ancient steps. One ominous night they supported our Lord's feet as he climbed with his accusers to the high priest's courtyard.

Several important discoveries help verify the authenticity of this site. The deep pit or dungeon, along with the adjacent guard room and public prison, attests that the house belonged to a prominent political leader. The existence of servants' quarters and a grain cellar suggest a wealthy owner.

The most significant find proved to be a large, heavy door lintel. The Hebrew inscription *Le acham hou Korban* ("This is the Korban for sin offerings") graces it. The Hebrew word *Korban* means "sacrifice" (see Mark 7:11). According to the Law, the trespass and sin offerings were not brought into the Temple. The priests kept them (Leviticus 7:7, 2 Kings 12:16). In addition to the revealing inscription, special measuring jars for liquids and solids used only by the priests were unearthed. This important discovery confirmed the prior conjecture that this was indeed the residence of the high priest.

After Judas' betrayal in the Garden of Gethsemane, Temple Guards arrested Jesus and escorted him to this house (Luke 22:54). It was likely past 11:00 p.m. by the time the detachment arrived with their prisoner. John records that Annas, the father-in-law and predecessor of Caiaphas, conducted the first inquiry (John 18:13). As "high priest emeritus," Annas exercised significant influence and control over the Sanhedrin, the highest Jewish tribunal.

Following this brief interview, Caiaphas and the chief officials of the Sanhedrin launched a preliminary investigation seeking sufficient evidence against Jesus to obtain a death sentence (Mark 14:55). All the Gospel accounts make it clear that this clandestine inquest resulted in the charge that Jesus claimed to be the Son of God, a blasphemy

A mosaic on the south side of the church graphically depicts the manner in which Jesus was lowered into the high priest's dungeon.

Ancient store houses and grain silos uncovered at the base of the church attest to the fact that the first century mansion was home to an important political and/or religious figure.

House of Caiaphas

meriting the death penalty (Numbers 15:30-31). As required by Jewish law, if blasphemy is proved, the judges respond by standing up and rending their garments, ". . . and they may not mend them again" (Mishnah, *Sanhedrin* 7:5).

The high priest's timing proved awkward; he could not formally try Jesus until daybreak. By law, capital cases must be tried and the verdict reached during the daytime (Mishnah, *Sanhedrin* 4:1). Since he could take no official action for at least six hours, Caiaphas imprisoned Jesus in his basement dungeon until dawn. He was blindfolded and beaten (Luke 22:63-65). His bleeding wounds would be washed with brine ("pouring salt into the wound"). Jesus endured an agonizing night of abuse and abandonment in the high priest's dark dungeon.

Directly above the dungeon, in the outer courtyard, another spiri-

The entrance to the Church of St. Peter in Gallicantu.

The Stones Cry Out

tual battle progressed. Peter initially displayed great courage. While the other disciples forsook their Lord and fled, Peter and an unnamed disciple (probably John) followed Jesus to the high priest's house. The trauma of that fateful night, however, eventually demoralized Peter, gripping him with fear. During his all-night vigil, Peter, in dialogue with three individuals, denied knowing Jesus. Heralding the foreboding dawn, the cry of the rooster reminded Peter of his Lord's prophecy — ". . . 'Before the rooster crows today, you will disown me three times.' And he went outside and wept bitterly" (Luke 22:61-62).

Isaiah, the prophet of redemption, foresaw these singular events of apparent defeat and ultimate victory. It is more than coincidence that the name *Isaiah* ("Salvation of Jehovah") is almost identical in meaning with *Joshua* ("Jehovah is Salvation") which appears in the New Testament as *Jesus*. In one of the best-loved chapters in all the Bible, the prophet reminds us that the Messiah's suffering achieves our salvation — "But he was wounded for our transgressions, he was bruised for our iniquities: the chastisement of our peace was upon him; and with his stripes we are healed" (Isaiah 53:5 KJV).

With Peter, may we forever ". . . rejoice that (we) participate in the sufferings of Christ, so that (we) may be overjoyed when his glory is revealed" (1 Peter 4:13).

Below left: Jesus spent an agonizing night in the dungeon of the high priest's home.

Below right: Jesus doubtless climbed this section of a first century terrace street leading to Caiaphas' house on the night of his arrest in the Garden of Gethsamane.

Via Dolorosa

A street sign in Hebrew, Arabic and English marks the Via Dolorosa — "The Way of Sorrow."

The last two chapters differ from the others in that they focus on sites disputed by scholars. Previous chapters have focused on locations authenticated to varying degrees by archaeological and historic evidence. The exact location of the events commemorated along the Via Dolorosa (including the site of Jesus' crucifixion and burial) are in question. Therefore, we will concentrate on the facts and significance of each incident rather then its precise location.

The Via Dolorosa is Christendom's most hallowed road. Winding along narrow streets of the Christian Quarter in Jerusalem's Old City, the "Way of Sorrow" leads from the Ecce Homo Convent to the Church of the Holy Sepulchre. This is the traditional route Jesus followed, bearing his cross from Pilate's judgment hall in the Antonia Fortress to Golgotha, site of the crucifixion. As early as the fourth century, processions from Gethsemane to Golgotha followed approximately the same route traveled by pilgrims today.

Fourteen "Stations of the Cross" commemorate events taking place along this agonizing, sorrowful walk. The Gospels describe eight of the events; the remaining six are tradition as taught by the Roman Catholic Church. The first two took place within the site of the Antonia Fortress, seven occurred in the streets, and the last five stations are within the Church of the Holy Sepulchre.

The Roman Catholic Church does not claim that each station marks the exact location of the event commemorated. Instead, they are sites where the Church venerates an event based on the Gospel accounts or Church tradition.

The pilgrimage begins in the Praetorium, the site of the Antonia Fortress that guarded the northern side of the Temple Mount in Jesus' day. The fortress was headquarters for the Roman garrison stationed in Jerusalem and served as residence of the procurator when he visited

Fourteen "Stations of the Cross" form the Via Dolorosa. Station number three commemorates when Jesus fell under the cross for the first time.

Stones of the Lithostroton, a large pavement found under the Ecce Homo Convent, believed by some to be the pavement of the Praetorium. Roman soldiers carved the gameboard of the "Game of the Kings" in the pavement stones. The soldiers played this game in association with scourging a condemned prisoner before crucifixion.

Ecce Homo Arch spans the beginning of the Via Dolorosa. The name means "Behold the Man." Many believe that under this arch, below the present street level, Pontius Pilate presented Christ to the jeering crowds (John 19:5).

Jerusalem. It was to this Praetorium ("fortress") Roman soldiers delivered Jesus for trial before the procurator, Pontius Pilate. This took place during the fateful Feast of Passover of the year 30 A.D.

Deep beneath the Ecce Homo Convent lies a large red stone courtyard which many believe to be the very pavement on which Jesus was condemned. John refers to this location as the "place that is called the Pavement (*lithostroton*), but in the Hebrew, Gabbatha" (John 19:13, KJV). The two words, as John implies, have different meanings. *Lithostroton* means "paved place," and *gabbatha* means "raised place." It is likely that the Romans erected a platform in an outdoor paved area of the Antonia Fortress. From this "judgment seat" the resident procurator made his public appearances and conducted trials.

This was the scene of Jesus' public trial. Pontius Pilate presented

Above left: The Antonia Fortress (center left) towers over the sacred Temple Mount in this reconstruction of first century Jerusalem at the Holyland Hotel.

Above right: Standing on the northeast corner of the Temple Mount or Harah esh-Sharif (present day courtyard to The Dome of the Rock) one can see where The Antonia Fortress stood in Jesus' day. Little remains of the fortress (Praetorium) itself. The compound where it stood is now occupied by the Al'Omariyeh College (pictured to the right of and including the minaret) and was formerly a Turkish army barracks.

Jesus scourged to the mocking crowd and said, "Behold the man" (*Ecce Homo*, in Latin). Pilate was not convinced that Jesus was guilty of any crime. He had hoped that the scourging would placate the Jewish leaders, but they shrewdly reminded him that Jesus claimed to be a king. Such a claim made him an enemy of Tiberius Caesar, the emperor (John 19:12-13). When Pilate realized that he ". . . was getting nowhere, but that instead an uproar was starting, he took water and washed his hands in front of the crowd. . . and handed him over to be crucified" (Matthew 27:24-26).

Still remaining today, faintly etched in the ancient pavement stones, are traces of games played by the Roman soldiers. This could be the dice game called "the King's Game" used by the soldiers with Jesus (Matthew 27:27-30, Mark 15:16-20). As part of this bizarre amusement, the soldiers chose a burlesque king, mocked and flogged him. At the end of the "game" they led the debilitated prisoner to the place of crucifixion.

Of the remaining seven stations in the streets of Old Jerusalem, only two commemorate an event recorded in scripture. Station Five commemorates the point at which the soldiers forced Simon the Cyrenian to carry the cross (Mark 15:21). Station Eight recalls the time Jesus paused to console the women of Jerusalem (Luke 23:27-31).

The distinctive grey-domed Church of the Holy Sepulchre stands in the center of the Christian Quarter of the Old City. It is visited each year by thousands of pilgrims from around the world. Many believe that it houses the place called Golgotha and the tomb where Jesus was laid after his crucifixion.

The Stones Cry Out

Three marble pillars flank the double arched gateway to the Church of the Holy Sepulchre. The Crusaders built the entrance in the early twelfth century A.D. The portal to the right was blocked by the conquering Sultan Saladin in 1187 A.D.

The Via Dolorosa ends within the walls of the Church of the Holy Sepulchre, one of the oldest and revered Christian churches. This ancient basilica houses what many believe to be the tomb where Jesus was laid following his crucifixion. The church also encloses a possible location for the ". . . place called Golgotha, that is to say, a place of a skull" (Matthew 27:33, KJV).

The Church of the Holy Sepulchre is unique in that it is divided among six Christian communities — Greek Orthodox, Armenians, Franciscans, Ethiopians, Copts and Syrian Jacobites. Each group zealously protects its rights and, if possible, attempts to extend them. Not until 1957 did the various communities manage to cooperate in a restoration project that is yet to be completed.

The next chapter will consider an alternate location for Golgotha and the tomb belonging to Joseph of Arimathea. Since human tendency is to worship the creation instead of the Creator, it is well that the site of our Lord's death and burial remains a mystery. If the precise location were known, the inclination would be to worship the site instead of the Savior.

The Via Dolorosa is believed to be the path taken by Jesus when he carried the cross to the place of crucifixion. There is little difference between the narrow, crowded shop-lined streets of today and those of Jerusalem in the first century A.D.

Whether standing in front of the elaborate Stations Eleven, Twelve and Thirteen in the Church of the Holy Sepulchre, or surveying Gordon's Calvary adjacent to the crowded, noisy bus station near the Damascus Gate, one confronts the *fact* of our Lord's undeserved, but willing, death.

Whether stooping low to enter the ancient crypt for which the Holy Sepulchre is named, or standing in the pastoral setting of the Garden Tomb, the *truth* of Christ's glorious resurrection quickens the believer's heart. In both empty first-century tombs, the angelic proclamation to Mary Magdalene and the other women takes on added meaning — **"HE HAS RISEN! HE IS NOT HERE"** (Mark 16:6).

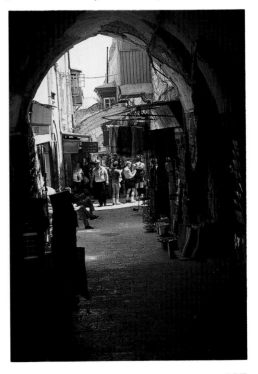

Gordon's Calvary and the Garden Tomb

Visitors to Jerusalem are surprised to find two very different sites commemorating the death, burial and resurrection of Jesus. Many Protestants believe that Gordon's Calvary and the Garden Tomb, located in a tranquil garden outside the Old City walls, is the site of Jesus' crucifixion and burial. The Roman Catholic Church, on the other hand, recognizes the Church of the Holy Sepulchre inside the crowded Christian Quarter of the Old City as the actual site of Calvary and Joseph of Arimathea's tomb.

General Charles George Gordon, a notable British military hero, came to Jerusalem in 1883 to meditate and renew his faith. Soon after his arrival he identified a hill outside the northern wall of the Old City as the site of Golgotha — in Aramaic, "skull" (Matthew 27:33, Mark 15:22, John 19:17). Although General Gordon was not the first to associate Skull Hill with the crucifixion, it has become known as "Gordon's Calvary."

On January 20, 1883 General Gordon wrote to a friend in England. "You have the ordnance map of Jerusalem. Look at the shape of the contour Number 2459 — Jeremiah's Grotto, near Damascus Gate. It is the shape of a skull; near it are gardens and caves, and close to it are the shambles of Jerusalem. . . To me, this Jeremiah Grotto area was the site of the crucifixion. Others also have said so."

Jeremiah's Grotto is located on the main road leading north to Damascus. According to Jewish tradition, the prophet Jeremiah wrote his Lamentations while living in a cave of this ancient quarry. Christian tradition also claims this as the site where Stephen, the first Christian martyr, was stoned to death.

While the actual site of the crucifixion is not certain, the location of the cross in relation to the surrounding terrain is generally accepted. George Bennard's popular hymn notwithstanding, it is unlikely the Old Rugged Cross stood *"on* a hill." The New Testament does not picture *Golgotha* (Aramaic) or *Calvary* (Latin) as a hill. It is described as a *place* called "the

In 1883 this ancient quarry hill was identified by General Charles Gordon as Golgotha, site of the crucifixion. The unique shape of the hill conforms to the New Testament description of Golgotha as "the place of a skull" (John 19:17). The precipice also conceals a vast underground cemetery.

The Stones Cry Out

The Garden Tomb is located in a beautifully kept garden just north of the Damascus Gate. The Garden Tomb Association maintains the tomb and surrounding garden. For many thousands who annually visit this tranquil spot, the Garden Tomb is a pilgrimage highlight.

place of the Skull (which in Aramaic is called Golgotha)" (John 19:17). Execution crosses no doubt were erected somewhere at the foot of the hill, on level ground and close to the busy highway.

The Romans used this brutal method of execution as a deterrent. They wanted those who passed by to read the accusation printed above each malefactor. They encouraged the crowd that had gathered to taunt, ridicule and humiliate the condemned criminal (Matthew 27:39). The Roman writer Quintillian in his *Declarations* made clear the purpose of crucifixion. He wrote, "Wherever we crucify criminals, very crowded highways are chosen so that many may see it, and many may be moved by fear of it."

Only a few hundred feet from Skull Hill is a rock-cut sepulchre known today as the Garden Tomb. It was first discovered in 1867 by a peasant trying to cultivate the land. An ancient cistern, found not far from the tomb, confirmed that the area once had been a garden. The shape of the nearby hill, the burial cave and the ancient garden fit the

A tour group at the Garden Tomb.

New Testament description. In 1893 a British interdenominational group called The Garden Tomb Association purchased the one-acre site. The association's sole purpose was "the preservation of the Tomb and Garden, outside the Walls of Jerusalem, believed by many to be the Sepulchre and Garden of Joseph of Arimathea."

The question remains — "Is the Garden Tomb or the Holy Sepulchre Church the actual location of the Lord's borrowed grave?" While there is sound, logical argument in favor of both sites, religious pride and prejudice caused deep division among well-meaning Christian groups for decades. In recent years, however, there has been a more enlightened approach to the controversy. A Roman Catholic priest's recent visit to the Garden Tomb underscores this new understanding. After receiving permission to celebrate mass with his tour group, he was asked why he had brought his group to the Garden Tomb. He readily replied, "I think I ought to explain that we *know* the Holy Sepulchre is *the* place, but we think it must have looked like this!"

The events of Resurrection Sunday come to life in the serene pastoral setting of the Garden Tomb. With little effort one can picture Mary Magdalene visiting the empty tomb "early, when it was yet dark" (John 20:1, KJV). She must have arrived before 6:00 a.m. since the word used for "early" is *proi*, a technical word meaning the last of the four night watches — 3:00 to 6:00 a.m.

An ancient cistern discovered near the Garden Tomb revealed that the area had been a garden in antiquity.

An old quarry northeast of the Damascus Gate overlooks a raucous city bus station. Many Christians believe this to be the site of Christ's crucifixion. The outcrop of rock forms the northern extent of Mount Moriah (Temple Mount). King Solomon used rocks from this quarry to build the First Temple.

Mary had been forgiven freely, and she freely loved. Oh, how she loved the Man who did for her what no other could ever do! In her grief, she no doubt observed the custom of visiting a loved one's tomb for three days after burial. The spirit of the dead person was believed to linger near the body for three days before departing.

Arriving at the tomb early Sunday morning, Mary and the women with her were stunned and frightened. The massive spherical stone that the authorities had sealed (Matthew 27:66) had been removed! Unable to face this themselves, they returned to the city to find Peter and John. In a breathless race, John reached the tomb first. He looked in but hesitated to go further. Impetuous Peter hurried inside.

John noticed that the grave clothes were not thrown aside. They were lying on the rock ledge, as the Greek word implies, "still in their folds." It was as if Jesus had simply vanished out of them! John at once understood the meaning of this supernatural, cataclysmic event — "He saw and believed" (John 20:8).

Inside the Garden Tomb is a sepulchral chamber on the right containing two burial places. The sepulchre to the left is considered by many to be the grave where Jesus was buried and rose again.

Understandably in a hurry to spread the good news, Peter and John rushed off, leaving Mary weeping outside the sepulchre's entrance. Peering into the tomb, Mary saw two angels in white who asked her why she was weeping. Her sorrowful reply still echoed through the crypt when Jesus approached from behind asking the same question. Through her sorrow and tears Mary could not recognize Jesus' voice or face — that is, until he called her by name.

Two millennia later, those who carefully listen will also recognize the Master's voice tenderly pleading — ". . . I stand at the door and knock. If anyone hears my voice and opens the door, I will come in and eat with him, and he with me" (Revelation 3:20).

Appendix

The Kingdoms of Israel and Judah

This map is printed with the permission of World Bible Publishers, Inc.

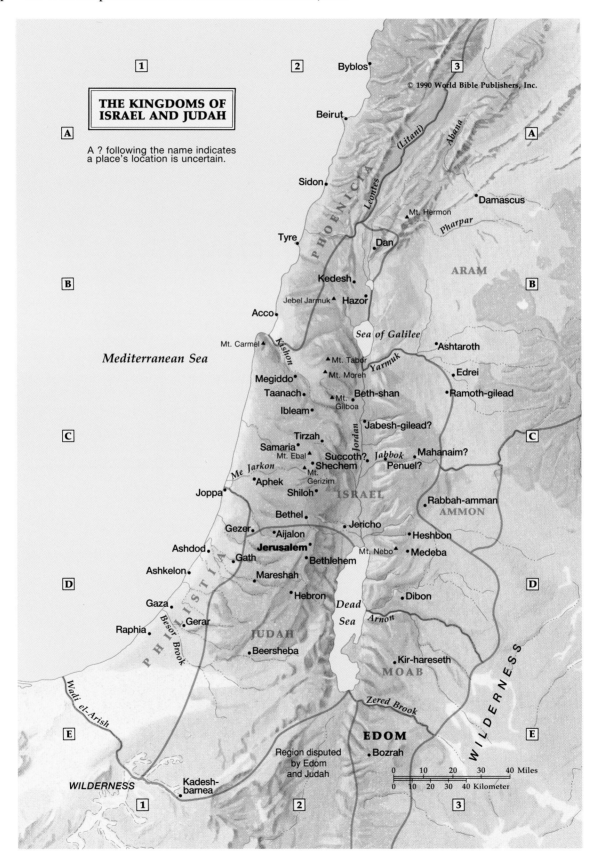

THE KINGDOMS OF
ISRAEL AND JUDAH

A ? following the name indicates
a place's location is uncertain.

© 1990 World Bible Publishers, Inc.

Byblos

Beirut

Sidon

Tyre

Kedesh

Acco

Jebel Jarmuk ▲ Hazor

Mt. Carmel ▲

Mediterranean Sea

Megiddo
Taanach
Ibleam

Tirzah
Samaria
Mt. Ebal ▲
Shechem
Mt. Gerizim ▲

Me Jarkon
Aphek
Shiloh

Joppa

Bethel

Gezer
Aijalon
Ashdod
Jerusalem
Gath
Bethlehem
Ashkelon
Mareshah

Gaza
Hebron
Gerar
Raphia
JUDAH
Beersheba

PHILISTIA

Wadi el-Arish

WILDERNESS

Kadesh-barnea

Leontes (Litani)

Abana

▲ Mt. Hermon

Dan

Pharpar

Damascus

ARAM

Sea of Galilee

▲ Mt. Tabor
▲ Mt. Moreh

Yarmuk

Ashtaroth

Edrei

Beth-shan
▲ Mt. Gilboa

Ramoth-gilead

Jabesh-gilead?

Jordan

Succoth? *Jabbok*
Penuel?

Mahanaim?

ISRAEL

Jericho

Rabbah-amman

AMMON

Heshbon

Mt. Nebo ▲ Medeba

Dead Sea

Dibon

Arnon

Kir-hareseth

MOAB

Zered Brook

EDOM

Bozrah

Region disputed
by Edom
and Judah

0   10   20   30   40 Miles
0 10 20 30 40 Kilometer

W I L D E R N E S S

114

The Stones Cry Out

Ministry of Jesus

This map is printed with the permission of World Bible Publishers, Inc.

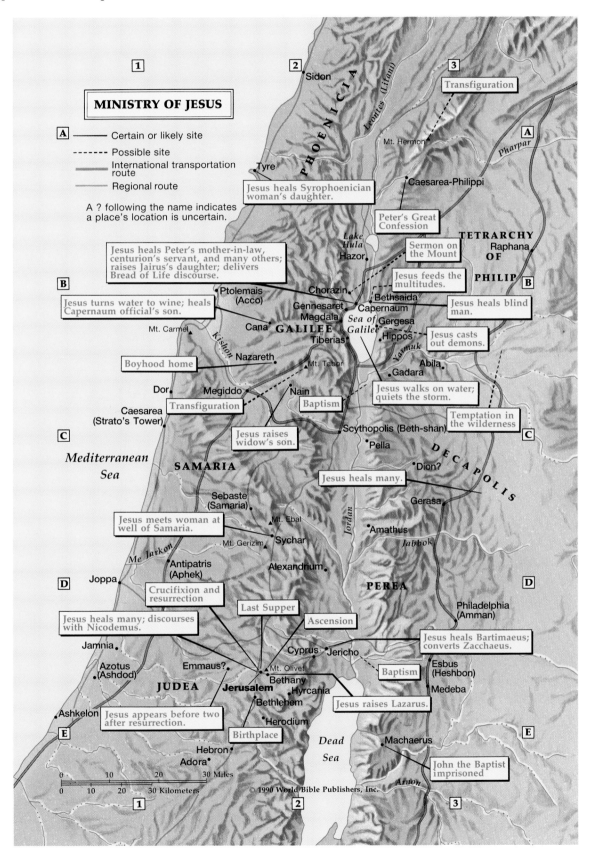

New Testament Jerusalem

This map is printed with the permission of World Bible Publishers, Inc.

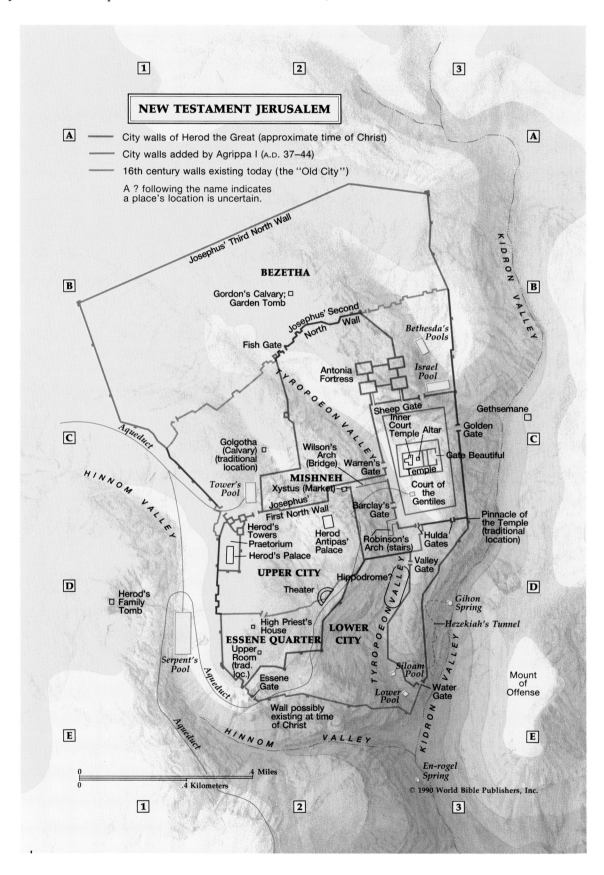

NEW TESTAMENT JERUSALEM

— City walls of Herod the Great (approximate time of Christ)

— City walls added by Agrippa I (A.D. 37–44)

— 16th century walls existing today (the "Old City")

A ? following the name indicates a place's location is uncertain.

Josephus' Third North Wall

BEZETHA

Gordon's Calvary; Garden Tomb

Josephus' Second North Wall

Fish Gate

Bethesda's Pools

KIDRON VALLEY

Antonia Fortress

Israel Pool

Sheep Gate

Inner Court Temple   Altar

Gethsemane

Golden Gate

TYROPOEON VALLEY

Aqueduct

Golgotha (Calvary) (traditional location)

Wilson's Arch (Bridge)   Warren's Gate

Temple

Gate Beautiful

MISHNEH

Xystus (Market)

Court of the Gentiles

HINNOM VALLEY

Tower's Pool

Josephus' First North Wall

Barclay's Gate

Pinnacle of the Temple (traditional location)

Herod's Towers   Praetorium

Herod Antipas' Palace

Robinson's Arch (stairs)

Hulda Gates

Herod's Palace

Valley Gate

UPPER CITY

Hippodrome?

Theater

Herod's Family Tomb

High Priest's House

ESSENE QUARTER   LOWER CITY

Upper Room (trad. loc.)

Gihon Spring

Hezekiah's Tunnel

Serpent's Pool

TYROPOEON VALLEY

Essene Gate

Siloam Pool

KIDRON VALLEY

Aqueduct

Mount of Offense

Lower Pool

Water Gate

Wall possibly existing at time of Christ

HINNOM VALLEY

Aqueduct

En-rogel Spring

| 0 | .4 Miles |
| 0 | .4 Kilometers |

© 1990 World Bible Publishers, Inc.

Herod and His Descendants

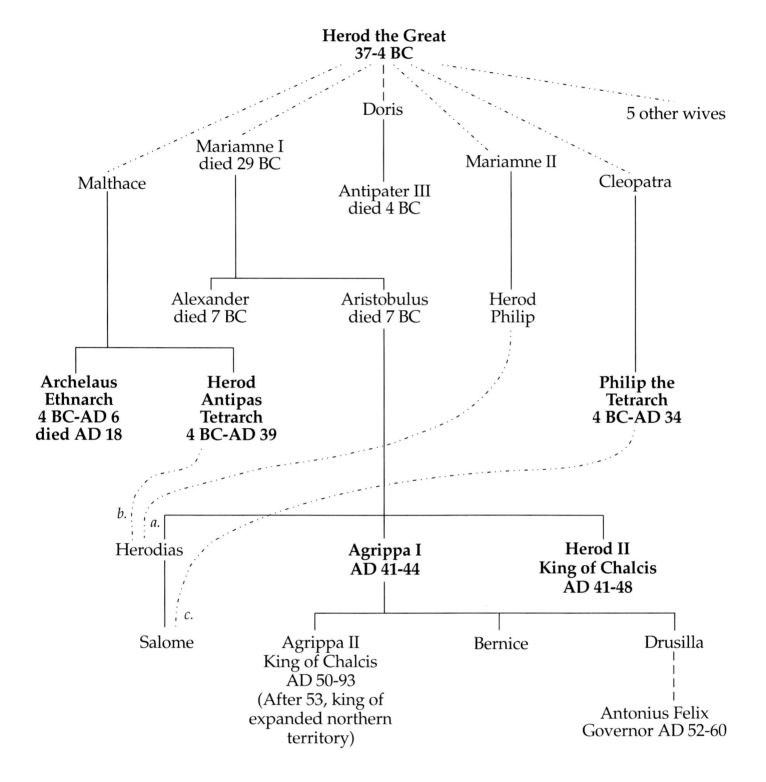

Herod the Great
37-4 BC

Doris

5 other wives

Mariamne I
died 29 BC

Malthace

Mariamne II

Cleopatra

Antipater III
died 4 BC

Alexander
died 7 BC

Aristobulus
died 7 BC

Herod
Philip

**Archelaus
Ethnarch
4 BC-AD 6
died AD 18**

**Herod
Antipas
Tetrarch
4 BC-AD 39**

**Philip the
Tetrarch
4 BC-AD 34**

b.

a.

Herodias

**Agrippa I
AD 41-44**

**Herod II
King of Chalcis
AD 41-48**

c.

Salome

Agrippa II
King of Chalcis
AD 50-93
(After 53, king of
expanded northern
territory)

Bernice

Drusilla

Antonius Felix
Governor AD 52-60

Married ·······-·-·-·-·-

a. First marriage of Herodias.

b. Second marriage of Herodias.

c. Salome, the daughter of Heridias and
   Herod (also referred to as Philip), danced
   before Herod Antipas for John the Baptist's
   head. She married her great-uncle Philip
   the Tetrarch.

Temple Mount of Herod the Great

Ritmeyer, Leen. "**The Temple Mount of Herod the Great**" (No. 32). Skelton, England: Ritmeyer Archaeological Design.

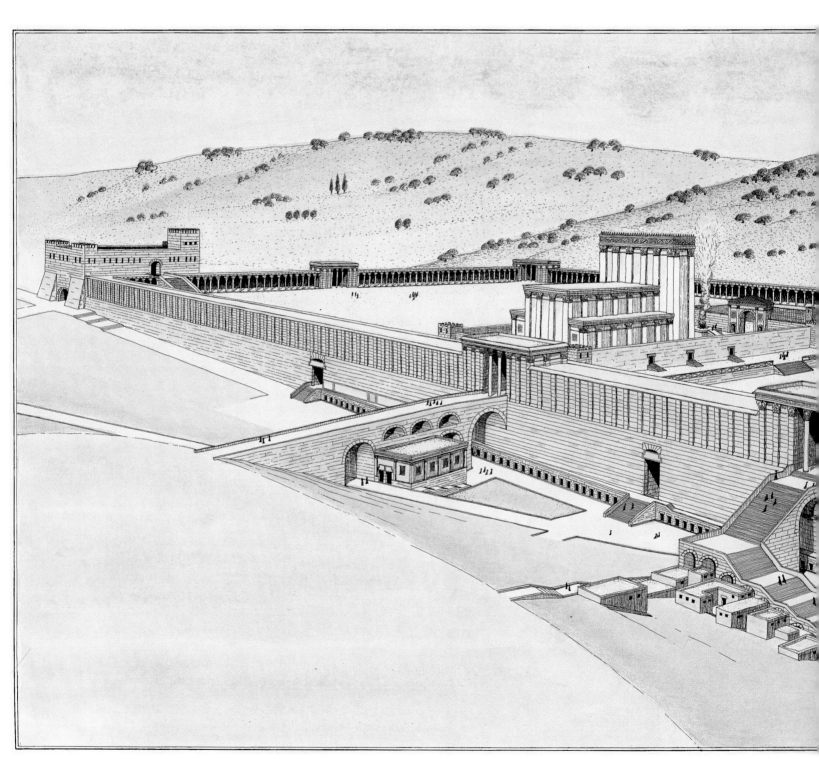

© L. RITMEYER

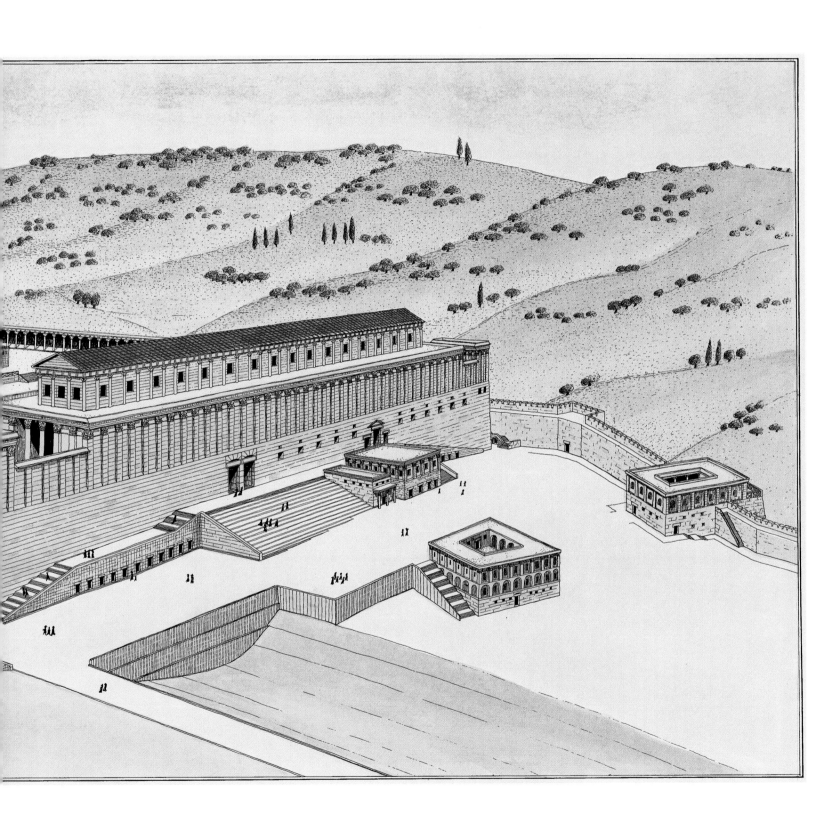

Jerusalem in 30 A.D.

Ritmeyer, Leen. "**The City During 30 A.D.**" (No. 31). Skelton, England: Ritmeyer Archaeological Design.

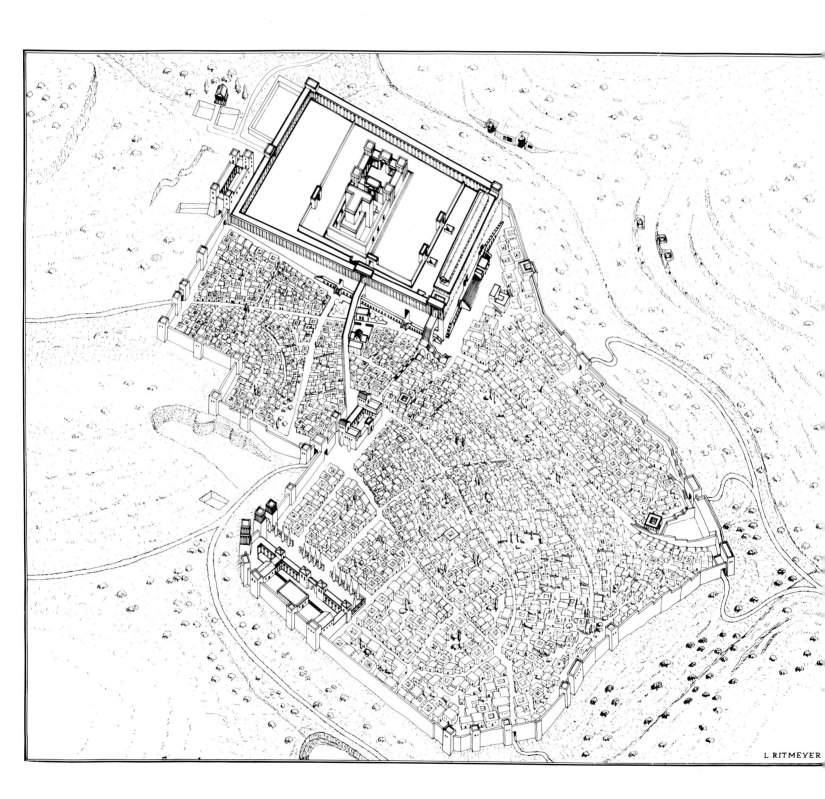

L. RITMEYER

The Stones Cry Out

Archaeological Sites

Frank, Harry Thomas, ed. "Archaeological Sites in Israel and Jordan." *Atlas of the Bible Lands.* Maplewood, New Jersey: Hammond Incorporated, 1984: B-38.

Miracles of Jesus

Miracle by location	Matthew	Mark	Luke	John	Site
In Capernaum - (12)					
Official's son				4:46-54	Official's house
Man possessed		1:23-28	4:33-37		Synagogue
Peter's mother-in-law	8:14-15	1:29-31	4:38-39		Peter's house
Paralyzed man	9:1-8	2:1-12	5:17-26		A house
Man with a shriveled hand	12:9-14	3:1-6	6:6-11		Synagogue
Centurion's servant	8:5-13		7:1-10		Centurion's house
Man blind, mute and possessed	12:22-24		(11:14-16)		Unspecified
Jairus' daughter	9:18-19 23-26	5:22-24 38-43	8:41-42 49-56		Jairus' house
Woman with hemorrhage	9:20-22	5:25-34	8:43-48		City streets
Two blind men	9:27-31				A house
Man mute and possessed	9:32-34				Outside the house
Coin in the fish's mouth	17:24-27				Capernaum shore
Around the Sea of Galilee - (6)					
Man with leprosy	8:1-4	1:40-45	5:12-16		Between Mount of Beatitudes & Capernaum
Two men from Gergesa	8:28-34	5:1-20	8:26-39		Gergesa (Kursi)
Feeding of the 5,000	14:15-21	6:34-44	9:12-17	6:5-13	Bethsaida suburbs
Deaf mute		7:31-37			Unspecified
Feeding of the 4,000	15:32-38	8:1-9			NE Shore
Blind man		8:22-26			Bethsaida
On the Sea of Galilee - (4)					
Catch of fish			5:1-11		Tabgha Shore
Calming the storm	8:23-27	4:35-41	8:22-25		Between Capernaum and Gergesa
Walking on the sea	14:22-32	6:47-51		6:16-21	Between NE shore and Capernaum
Large catch of fish (153)				21:1-11	Tabgha Shore
In Jerusalem (5)					
Invalid man				5:1-15	Pool of Bethesda
Man blind from birth				9:1-41	Temple Area and Pool of Siloam
Stooped woman			13:10-17		A synagogue in or near Jerusalem
Man with dropsy			14:1-6		Pharisee's house
High priest's servant			22:47-51		Garden of Gethsamane

Miracle by location	Matthew	Mark	Luke	John	Site
At Other Locations (8)					
Water turned into wine				2:1-11	Cana
Widow's son			7:11-17		Nain
Canaanite woman's daughter	15:21-28	7:24-30			Tyre & Sidon
Epileptic boy	17:14-21	9:14-29	9:37-43a		Caesarea Philipi
Ten men with leprosy			17:11-19		Border of Galilee and Samaria
Two blind men (including Bartimaeus)	20:29-34	10:46-52	18:35-43		Jericho
Lazarus				11:1-44	Bethany
Fig tree withered	21:17-22	11:12-14	20-26		Bethpage

Summary of Miracles by Location

Capernaum	12
Sea of Galilee *	
- on shore	6
- on the sea	4
Jerusalem	5
Bethany	1
Bethpage	1
Caesarea Philipi	1
Cana	1
Galilee/Samaria border	1
Jericho	1
Nain	1
Tyre/Sidon	1
TOTAL	35

* The ten miracles performed *around* and *on* the Sea of Galilee (with the exception of those taking place in Capernaum) include:

Bethsaida	2
Gergesa	1
Shoreline	3
On the Sea	4

NOTE - Unspecified miracles were performed in Korazim and Bethsaida (northern shore of the Sea of Galilee) according to Matthew 11:21. Jesus also "healed many who were sick of various diseases. . ." in Capernaum (Matthew 8: 16-17, Mark 1:32-34, Luke 4:40-41).

Summary of Miracles by Book

Matthew	20
Mark	18
Luke	20
John	8

Parables of Jesus

Parable by location	Matthew	Mark	Luke	Site
In Capernaum - (13)				
The new cloth and old garment	9:16	2:21	5:36	Matthew's house
The two debtors			7:36-50	House of Simon the Pharisee
The new wine in old wineskins	9:17	2:22	5:37-39	House of Simon the Pharisee
The soils	13:1-9, 18-23	4:1-20	8:4-15	From a boat near shore
The weeds	13:24-30			From a boat near shore
	36-43			After return to house with disciples
The seed and fertile earth		4:26-29		From a boat near shore
The mustard seed	13:31-32	4:30-34	(13:18-19)	From a boat near shore
The leaven (yeast)	13:33		(13:20-21)	From a boat near shore
The hidden treasure	13:44			After return to house with disciples
The pearl of great price	13:45-46			After return to house with disciples
The dragnet	13:47-51			After return to house with disciples
The treasures old and new	13:52			After return to house with disciples
The unforgiving servant	18:23-35			A house
Around the Sea of Galilee - (2)				
The lamp under a bushel	5:14-16	(4:21-23)	8:16-17	Mountain near Capernaum —
			11:33-36	(Mount of Beatitudes)
The houses on rock and sand	7:24-27		6:46-49	Mountain near Capernaum
In Jerusalem (8)				
The friend calling at midnight			11:5-13	Near Jerusalem - (Trad. Mount of Olives)
The two sons	21:28-32			Temple Courts
The wicked tenants	21:33-46	12:1-12	20:9-19	Temple Courts
The wedding feast of the king's son	22:1-14			Temple Courts
The fig tree-herald of summer	24:32-33	13:28-29	21:29-32	Mount of Olives
The ten maidens	25:1-13			Mount of Olives
The talents (Matthew)	25:14-30			Mount of Olives
pounds (Luke)			19:12-27	Mount of Olives
The sheep and the goats	25:31-46			
At Other Locations (17)				
The good Samaritan			10:25-37	On the road to Jerusalem before reaching Bethany
The foolish rich man			12:13-21	Unspecified
The alert servants			12:35-40	Unspecified
The faithful steward			12:42-48	Unspecified
The unfruitful fig tree			13:6-9	Unspecified
The places of honor at wedding feast			14:7-14	Chief Pharisee's house on the sabbath

Parable by location	Matthew	Mark	Luke	Site
At Other Locations (continued)				
The great banquet			14:16-24	Chief Pharisee's house on the sabbath
The counting of the cost			14:28-33	Upon leaving Chief Pharisee's house
The lost sheep		(18:12-14)	15:1-7	Unspecified (Capernaum - Matthew)
The lost coin			15:8-10	Unspecified
The lost son			15:11-32	Unspecified
The dishonest steward			16:1-13	Unspecified
The rich man and Lazarus			16:19-31	Unspecified
The master and his servant			17:7-10	Unspecified
The widow and the judge			18:1-8	Unspecified
The Pharisee and the tax collector			18:9-14	Unspecified
The laborers in a vineyard	20:1-16			Judea (beyond the Jordan en route to Jerusalem)

Summary of Parables by Location

Capernaum	13
Around Sea of Galilee	2
Jerusalem	8
Other sites	17
TOTAL	40

Summary of Parables by Book

Matthew	22
Mark	8
Luke	29

Bible History Time Chart

Frank, Harry Thomas, ed. "Time Chart of Bible History." *Atlas of the Bible Lands.* Maplewood, New Jersey: Hammond Incorporated, 1984: B-40,41,42.

Time Chart of Bible History

DATE	PALESTINE	EGYPT	MESOPOTAMIA & PERSIA	ANATOLIA & SYRIA	GREECE & ROME
4000 BC	Neolithic culture (Jericho)	— First use of metal: copper and bronze —			
	Ghassulian culture c.3500	Hieroglyphic writing developed	Halaf culture		
			Cuneiform writing developed		
	The Canaanites, a Semitic people, were ancestral to the Phoenicians	**Archaic Period** Menes unifies Egypt	Sumerian city states c.2800-2360	Early Bronze cities Byblos, Troy, Ugarit	Beginning of Minoan civilization on Crete
	Early Bronze urban culture c.3300	**Old Kingdom** The Great Pyramids at Gizeh c.2550	**Akkadian Empire** Sargon I 2360-2305	Syria under Akkadian Empire	
	Amorite invasions c.2500-2300	Old Kingdom falls	Gutian kings Ur dominance	Hittites enter Anatolia	Greeks invade Balkan peninsula
2000 BC	Egypt controls Canaan	**Middle Kingdom**	Ur falls c.1950 **Isin-Larsa Period** **Old Babylonian Empire**	Amorite invasions	**Minoan Sea Empire**
	Abraham — oral tradition	Hyksos invaders from Asia c.1720-1550	Hammurabi 1728-1686	Hittites intro. Iron Labarnas I c.1600	
	Israelite sojourn in Egypt		**Kassite Period** Hittites sack Babylon 1531	**Old Hittite Kingdom**	Mycenae shaft graves
	Battle of Megiddo 1468 Amarna letters c.1370-1353	**New Kingdom** Akhenaton 1370-1353 Tutankhamen 1353-1344	Mitanni Kdm.	Mursilis I c.1540	Cretan palaces destroyed c.1400
	The Exodus c.1290 Israelite invasion	Ramses II 1290-1224 Ramses III defeats Sea Peoples c.1170	**Rise of Assyria** Shalmaneser I	Suppilullumas **Hittite Empire**	Dorians invade Greece
	Philistine penetration Kdm. of Saul c.1020-1000	**Late Dynastic Period**	Tiglath-pileser I 1115-1078	Battle of Kedesh 1296 Sack of Troy 1192	Trojan War c.1200
1000 BC	**United Kingdom** David c.1000-961 Solomon c.961-922	Period of decline		Arameans flood into Syria	Decline of Aegean Bronze Age civilization
	First Temple completed c.950	Shishak c.935-914	**Assyrian Empire**	Hiram of Tyre 969-936 Damascus city state	Latins settle in central Italy
	Divided Kingdom Rehoboam & Jeroboam I	Libyan dynasties 950-710	Asshurnasirpal II 883-859	Ben-hadad II	
	Omri dynasty 876-842 Samaria founded c.875		Shalmaneser III 859-824	Battle of Qarqar 853	
	Jehu dynasty 842-745		Adad-nirari III 807-782	Phoenicians found Carthage 814	
800 BC	Israel resurgence under Jeroboam II 786-746 Amos, Hosea				First Olympics 776
	Fall of Samaria and exile of Israel 722/721		Tiglath-pileser III 745-727	Phrygian Kdm.	Legendary founding of Rome 753
	Hezekiah of Judah 715-687/6	Nubian dynasties 715-663	Sargon II 722-705 Sennacherib 705-681	Midas c.715	Etruscan period Homer
	Isaiah Micah Judah resurgence under Josiah 640-609 Jeremiah	Egypt under Assyrian rule 671-652 Thebes sacked 663 Neco II 609-593	Asshurbanapal 669-633 Rise of Babylon under Nabopolassar Fall of Nineveh to Medes and Babylonians 612	Lydian Kdm. Gyges of Lydia 680-652	Draco codifies Athenian law 621
600 BC					

Kings of Judah and Israel

JUDAH	ISRAEL	JUDAH	ISRAEL
Rehoboam 922-915 ●	● 922-901 Jeroboam I	Jotham 750-735 ●	● 746-745 Zechariah
Abijah 915-913 ●	● 901-900 Nadab		● 745 Shallum
Asa 913-873 ●	● 900-877 Baasha		● 745-738 Menahem
	● 877-876 Elah		● 738-737 Pekahiah
	● 876 Zimri	Ahaz 735-715 ●	● 737-732 Pekah
Jehoshaphat 873-849 ●	● 876-869 Omri		● 732-724 Hoshea
	● 869-850 Ahab	Hezekiah 715-687/6 ●	*722/721 Fall of Samaria*
	● 850-849 Ahaziah	Manasseh 687/6-642 ●	
Jehoram 849-842 ●	● 849-842 Jehoram	Amon 642-640 ●	
Ahaziah 842 ●	● 842-815 Jehu	Josiah 640-609 ●	
Athaliah 842-837 ●		Jehoahaz 609 ●	
Joash 837-800 ●	● 815-801 Jehoahaz	Jehoiakim 609-598 ●	
Amaziah 800-783 ●	● 801-786 Jehoash	Jehoiachin 598-597 ●	
Uzziah 783-742 ●	● 786-746 Jeroboam II	Zedekiah 597-587 ●	
		Fall of Jerusalem 587	

DATE	PALESTINE	EGYPT	MESOPOTAMIA & PERSIA	ANATOLIA & SYRIA	GREECE & ROME
600 BC	Destruction of Jerusalem and exile of Judah 587 Ezekiel **Babylonian Captivity** Edict of Cyrus allows return of Jews 538 Zerubbabel Temple rebuilt 520-515 **Persian Period** Ezra's mission 458?? Nehemiah comes to Judah 445 (440?)	Egypt under Persian rule 525-401 Unsuccessful revolt Return to native rule	**New Babylonian Empire** Nebuchadnezzar II 605-562 **Persian Empire** Cyrus 550-530 Babylon falls 539 Cambyses 530-522 Darius I 522-486 Xerxes I 486-465 Artaxerxes I Darius II 433-404	Syria and Anatolia under Persian rule Phoenicians provide fleet for Persian attacks on Greece	Solon's judicial reforms c.590 Rome ruled by Etruscan kings Roman Republic established 509 Persian Wars 499-479 Thermopylae-Salamis 480 Pericles 461-429 Herodotus
400 BC	Ezra's mission 398? Palestine passes under Alexander's rule and Hellenization begins 332 Ptolemaic Egyptian rule 312	Persian rule 342-332 Alexander conquers Egypt 332 Ptolemy I 323-284 **Ptolemaic Kingdom** Alexandrian Jews translate Pentateuch into Greek Ptolemy V 203-181	Artaxerxes III 358-338 Alexander invades Persia 331 Seleucid rule Parthians and Bactrians gain independence c.250	Alexander takes Tyre 332 Seleucid rule Seleucus I 312-280 **Seleucid Empire** Antiochus I 280-261 Seleucus II 246-226 Antiochus III (The Great) 223-187	Socrates' death Sack of Rome by Gauls Philip II of Macedon Alexander the Great 336-323 **Alexander's Empire** Wars of the Diodochi 1st and 2nd Punic Wars Hannibal in Italy 218
200 BC	Palestine comes under Seleucid Syrian control 198 **Maccabean Period** Judas Maccabeus leads revolt of Jews 166-160 Temple rededicated 164 Jonathan 160-142 Simon 142-134 John Hyrcanus I 134-104 Aristobulus I 104-103	Ptolemy VI 181-146 Antiochus IV campaigns in Egypt Ptolemy VII 146-116	**Parthian Empire** Mithridates I 171-138 Mithridates II 124-88	Battle of Magnesia 190 Antiochus IV (Epiphanes) 175-163 Antiochus V 163-162 Demetrius I 162-150 Demetrius II 145-139 Tyre independent	Spain annexed by Rome **Empire of the Roman Republic** 3rd Punic War Romans destroy Carthage and Corinth 146 Reforms of the Gracchi
100 BC **50 BC**	Alexander Jannaeus 103-76 Alexandra 76-67 Aristobulus II 67-63 Pompey takes Jerusalem for Rome 63 Hyrcanus II, high priest 63-40 Antipater governor 55	Ptolemy VIII 116-81 Ptolemy XI 80-81 Cleopatra VII 51-30	Tigranes of Armenia Phrates III 70-57 Orodes I 57-38 War with Rome 55-38 Crassus defeated	Mithridatic Wars Antiochus XIII 68-67 Anatolia and Syria under Roman control	Sulla dictator 82-79 1st Triumvirate Pompey's campaigns in Asia 66-63 Caesar's Gallic Wars 58-51

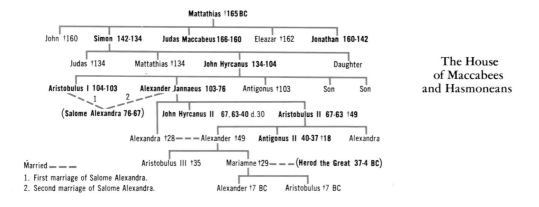

The House of Maccabees and Hasmoneans

Married — — —
1. First marriage of Salome Alexandra.
2. Second marriage of Salome Alexandra.

The Stones Cry Out

Time Chart of Bible History, Continued

DATE	PALESTINE	THE WEST	THE EAST
50 BC	**Roman Rule** Caesar in Judea 47 Parthian invasion 40 Antigonus 40-37 Herod the Great 37-4 BC Herod's Temple begun 18 Birth of Christ c.4 BC Archelaus 4 BC-AD 6	Death of Pompey 48 Death of Caesar 44 2nd Triumvirate Battle of Philippi 42 Battle of Actium 31 Augustus — First emperor 27 BC-AD 14 **Roman Empire**	**Parthian Empire** Phraates 37-32 Parthians defeat Antony 36
0	Roman governors 6-41 Pontius Pilate 27-37 Death of Christ c.29 Herod Agrippa I 41-44 Paul's 1st journey, Council at Jerusalem 46/47	Varus defeated in Germany 9 Tiberius 14-37 Gaius (Caligula) 37-41 Claudius 41-54 Conquest of Britain begun 43	Artabanus II 10-40
50 AD	Antonius Felix 52-60 Imprisonment of Paul 58 Porcius Festus 60-62 Paul sent to Rome 60 Gessius Florus 64-66 First Jewish Revolt 66-73 Destruction of Jerusalem 70 Fall of Masada 73 Jewish center at Jamnia	Nero 54-68 1st Persecution of Christians 64 Galba, Otho, Vitellius 68/69 Vespasian 69-79 Titus 79-81 Domitian 81-96 Nerva 96-98 Trajan 98-117	Vologases I 51-80 Parthian War with Rome 53-63 Osroes (Chosroes) 89-128
100 AD **135 AD**	Jewish uprisings in Palestine, Egypt, Mesopotamia 116-117 Bar-Kochba Revolt 132-135 Jerusalem razed, Aelia Capitolina built on site	Campaigns in Dacia 101-107 Hadrian 117-138	Conquest of Nabateans by Romans Trajan invades Parthia 114 Territory lost to Romans regained 118

Herod and His Descendants

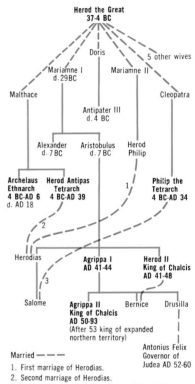

Married — — —
1. First marriage of Herodias.
2. Second marriage of Herodias.
3. Salome, daughter of Herodias and Herod (sometimes referred to as Philip), danced before Herod Antipas for John the Baptist's head. She married her great-uncle Philip the Tetrarch.

d. died

Roman catapult. A type of artillery used effectively by both Romans and Jews in the battle for Jerusalem, A.D. 69-70.

Index

Greek
architecture 73
cities 46
Empire 65
gods 53
language (words) 34, 92, 111
population 28
Greek Orthodox Church 11-12, 105

H

Hadrian, Emperor 6
Haggai, Prophet 72
Hajlah Ford (Jordan River) 17
Hashemite Kingdom of Jordan 17
Hasmonean Period 75, 96
Hebrew language (words) 3, 10, 13, 16, 24, 34, 46, 53, 59, 74, 78, 97, 103
Hebron 3
Helena, Queen 6
Heptapegon (See Tabgha)
Hermon
River 53
Mount 16, 20, 23, 25, 53, 56
Herod Antipas 23, 28
Herod the Great 28, 54, 66, 73-76
Herodian Period 74-76
Hesichios 2
Hezekiah, King 65, 79-80
tunnel 79-80
high priest 36, 71-72, 93, 96-99
Hippus 46-47
Hiram, King of Tyre 72
Holy of Holies (Debir) 71
Holy Spirit 19-20, 76, 84, 86-87
decent of the 84, 86-87
Hulda Gates 76
Huleh Valley 16, 25

I

Ibzan 4
irrigation 78
Isaac 31, 65, 71, 75
Isaiah, Prophet 12, 28, 84, 99
Ishmael 75
Islam 11, 60, 65, 71, 75, 85
Israel 11, 13, 16-18, 20, 30, 35, 53, 70, 71, 85
Israelites 4, 17
modern State of 17-18, 24, 75

Six Day War 48

J

Jabin, King 13
Jacob 3, 6, 31, 65
James, Apostle 34
Jebusites 66

Jeremiah, Prophet 108
Jericho 17, 18, 59
road 59
Jerusalem 2-3, 10-11, 17, 22, 41, 47, 56, 59, 62, 64-68, 70, 72, 74, 76, 78-80, 84-86, 90, 96, 102-104, 108, 110
Christian Quarter 102, 108
cisterns 78, 80
Damascus Gate 105, 108
daughters of 59
Dung Gate 71
Lion's Gate 78
Northern Wall 108
Old City 78, 85, 102
Sheep Gate 78
St. Stephen's Gate (Lion's Gate) 78
Jessie 4
Jesus
agony 91-93, 96, 98-99
arrest 90, 92-93
ascension 62, 84, 86, 90
atonement 86, 92
baptism 17-20
betrayal 90, 93, 97
birth 2-4, 6-7, 10
burial 12, 67, 102, 105, 108
childhood 10-12
crucifixion 16, 62, 67, 84, 92, 102, 104, 105, 108
disciples 11, 25, 34, 41-43, 54-56, 71, 76, 79, 80, 84, 86-87, 90-92
establishment of the church 86
feasts (attendance) 79
flogging 104
Last Supper 84, 86
life 16-17, 20, 25, 48, 67, 71, 76, 91, 93
Messiah 12, 18, 31, 55, 99
miracles 25, 29-31, 34-35, 47-50, 60-61, 67, 78-80, 82
mocking 104
name 7, 11, 67, 76, 99
Passion Week 84, 91
post-resurrection appearances 35, 37, 86
prayer 90, 92
religious leaders (confrontation) 67, 71, 79, 82
resurrection 62, 68, 105, 108, 110-111
return 62
scourging 104
Sermon on the Mount 40-43
Son of God 97
teachings 19, 25, 29-31, 34, 41-43, 48, 59
transfiguration 13, 56
trial 93, 97, 103
triumphal entry 91
Jewish Christians 76, 84, 87
Jewish Revolts 6, 74, 85
Jezreel Valley 10, 13, 56
Job, Spring of 34
John the Baptist 17-20, 61
Monastery of 17

The author's tour group poses for a picture on the Mount of Olives with the Dome of the Rock and Old City of Jerusalem in the background. Lt. Colonel and Mrs. Francis (right), along with their esteemed tour guide, Shabtai ("Shep") Levanon (left), enjoy a more elevated and animated view.

"Pray for the peace of Jerusalem: 'May those who love you be secure. May there be peace within your walls and security within your citadels.' "

-- Psalm 122:6

Fishermen on the Sea of Galilee.

Jesus may have alluded to the wild red anemone (buttercup family) that blankets the Holy Land in the Spring when he remarked, "And why do you worry about clothes? See how the lilies of the field grow. They do not labor or spin. Yet I tell you that not even Solomon in all his splendor was dressed like one of these" (Matthew 6:28-29).

The Stones Cry Out